a lifetime
of wisdom

Books by Joni Eareckson Tada

All God's Children: Ministry with Disabled Persons
(with Gene Newman)

Barrier-Free Friendships:
Bridging the Distance Between You and Friends with Disabilities
(with Steve Jensen)

Diamonds in the Dust: 366 Sparkling Devotions

The God I Love: A Lifetime of Walking with Jesus

Heaven: Your Real Home

Heaven: Devotional Edition

How to Be a Christian in a Brave New World
(with Nigel M. de S. Cameron)

Joni: An Unforgettable Story

The Life and Death Dilemma:
Families Facing Health Care Choices

More Precious Than Silver:
366 Daily Devotional Readings

Pearls of Great Price:
366 Daily Devotional Readings

A Step Further:
Growing Closer to God through Hurt and Hardship
(with Steven Estes)

When God Weeps:
Why Our Sufferings Matter to the Almighty
(with Steven Estes)

a lifetime of wisdom

embracing the way God heals you

Joni Eareckson Tada

ZONDERVAN.com/
AUTHORTRACKER
follow your favorite authors

ZONDERVAN

A Lifetime of Wisdom
Copyright © 2009 by Joni Eareckson Tada

Requests for information should be addressed to:

Zondervan, 3900 *Sparks Dr. SE, Grand Rapids, Michigan* 49546

This edition: ISBN 978-0-310-34683-8 (softcover)

Library of Congress Cataloging-in-Publication Data

Tada, Joni Eareckson.
    A lifetime of wisdom / Joni Eareckson Tada.
      p. cm.
    Includes bibliographical references.
    ISBN 978-0-310-27342-4
    1. Tada, Joni Eareckson. 2. Christian biography—United States. 3. Spiritual
life—Christianity. 4. Spirituality. 5. Christian life. I. Title.
BR1725.T2A3 2009
277.3'0825092—dc22
  [B]   2008036136

Published in association with the literary agency of Wolgemuth & Associates, Inc.

Interior design by Beth Shagene
Editorial assistant: Cassandra Gunn

First printing February 2016 / Printed in the United States of America

For Ken

Contents

The Price of Rubies

Job had maxed.

He'd taken just about all he could endure. As far as he could see, life was pretty much over.

> My *spirit is broken,*
>> *my days are cut short,*
>> *the grave awaits me. . . .*
> My *days have passed, my plans are shattered,*
>> *and so are the desires of my heart.*
>
> (Job 17:1, 11)

From words like these, it would be easy to conclude that the battered, grieving man had surrendered to complete despair, that he was so profoundly broken there could be no return to the sunlit lands.

But within the crisscrossing streams of words that form this real-life biblical drama, a wholly unexpected tributary knifes across the landscape. Several times in the midst of Job's grieving, complaining, and arguing with his four dubious comforters, the tone and content of his speech changes. It's almost as though he looks up through a tear in the cloud cover to see a fragment of blue sky—or perhaps a single star shining through a gap in the canopy.

> *Though he slay me, yet will I hope in him; . . .*
> *Indeed, this will turn out for my deliverance.*
>
> (Job 13:15, 16)

Does that sound like a man who has given up on life? From what source did these ringing words of hope spring? Job is saying, "Even though I may never understand why God has done what He has done, or why He has allowed these things to happen to me, He is worthy of my trust and my hope, and however this turns out, it will be for my salvation."

That was wisdom, and it didn't come easy.

It was insight, and it was hard-won.

They say if you're standing at the bottom of a deep well, you can look up in the middle of the day and see stars. I've never tried the experiment myself (I'll take their word for it), but it's clear to me that in the midst of the most horrendous experiences you can imagine, Job looked up toward heaven and saw things he had never seen before—or perhaps anyone had seen before.

> *Even now my witness is in heaven;*
> *my advocate is on high.*
> *My intercessor is my friend*
> *as my eyes pour out tears to God;*
> *on behalf of a man he pleads with God*
> *as a man pleads for his friend.*
>
> (Job 16:19–21)

A witness in heaven? *Who* would *that* be?

An intercessor and friend in God's presence who pleads Job's case? *Who* fits a description like *that*?

Who else could this be but Jesus? A few pages later, Job lifts his anguished face to heaven and cries out:

> *I know that my Redeemer lives,*
> *and that in the end he will stand upon the earth.*
> *And after my skin has been destroyed,*
> *yet in my flesh I will see God;*
> *I myself will see him*
> *with my own eyes—I, and not another.*
> *How my heart yearns within me!*
>
> (Job 19:25–27)

Job yearned for a glimpse behind the veil of pain and misery into the mysteries of a God he believed in and loved but had trouble trusting. After hearing his closest friends drag the remnants of his reputation across the hot coals of criticism, Job longed for some wisdom from above.

And he received it.

He wasn't given all he desired, and he could hardly process what he did receive in those stunning chapters of Job 38–41. Even so, he was given the privilege of peering into the treasuries of heaven. And although he wasn't permitted to gaze on those treasures directly, he saw flashes of their radiance by faith in his peripheral vision.

It wasn't the detailed explanation he hoped for (God never did get around to answering Job's "why" questions), but it was enough. Enough to sustain him. Enough to give him the perseverance to hang on through his suffering and endure.

Though he most likely lived in the early days of earth, before the New Testament, before Moses, and before Abraham, Job saw the Redeemer and the risen Lord—a flash of radiance in the deepest night. And he found comfort in what he saw. What's more (just think of it!), his words will *never* be lost, *never* die, *never* fade, because the Holy Spirit of God saw to it that they were inscribed in a document that would one day lie at the very heart of the Bible, the eternal Word of God. And here we are in the twenty-first century talking about them, just as we would discuss the morning's headlines on CNN or FOXNews.

Job was given wisdom. And that wisdom greatly exceeded our concept of value. In a later chapter, the broken man went on to describe just how precious such wisdom truly is.

> *But where can wisdom be found?*
> *Where does understanding dwell?*
> *Man does not comprehend its worth; . . . .*

> *It cannot be bought with the finest gold,*
> *nor can its price be weighed in silver. . . .*
> *the price of wisdom is beyond rubies.*
> (Job 28:12 – 13, 15, 18)

Have you ever seen rubies on display at a gem show or in a jewelry store? Picture for a moment a packing crate out in the middle of a sun-drenched field, filled to the brim with rubies, spilling over with rubies of every size, cut in a million intricate and perfect facets. How they would flash and sparkle, like scarlet fire! Imagine plunging your hand into that crate of rubies, bringing up a heaping handful, and letting the rare and precious stones—cool, smooth, and clean—spill through your fingers.

Very nice, says Job, a man who certainly knew all about wealth and how to appreciate the finer things of life. But if you have a choice, trade the whole box for true wisdom and never look back. "The price of wisdom is beyond rubies."

Job had paid dearly for his insights into the Person and nature of God, for those glimpses into eternal verities beyond the billowing curtain of time.

Centuries later, a king named Solomon would take a page out of Job's memoirs, writing,

> *Wisdom*
> *. . . is more profitable than silver*
> *and yields better returns than gold.*
> *She is more precious than rubies;*
> *nothing you desire can compare with her.*
> (Proverbs 3:13, 14 – 15)

Wisdom—insights into the nature of God and the ways of life—has more value than Bill Gates's bank account. It's more precious than the crown jewels of England, the treasures of the Louvre, and the hidden wealth of the Vatican. In fact, *nothing* compares with it.

It is beyond rubies, and yet, in the pages that follow (to give us something to see in our mind's eye), I will describe each of these breakthroughs in understanding as a splendid ruby.

But you don't find these gems at the bottom of a cereal box or enclosed in cellophane and tucked inside a Happy Meal. Many of them, perhaps most of them, come through long years of seeking God, waiting on God, and trusting Him through the most difficult and heartbreaking circumstances of life.

Skip forward in time to the prophet Jeremiah and his book of Lamentations. No one would call this part of Scripture a "happy read," and no one would be masochistic enough to want to live through what this good man endured in his lifetime. After God called him to warn and plead with the people of Judah to turn from their destructive ways, Jeremiah invested his whole career in that effort. As far as we know, no one ever responded, and Judah and Jerusalem were destroyed by the Babylonians anyway. The city was leveled and thousands lay slain and unburied in the streets. Thousands more marched off to Babylon in chains at the point of a spear.

Sitting on a hilltop, the prophet looked down at Ground Zero, his nostrils filled with drifting smoke from the ashes. Always a deeply sensitive man, Jeremiah poured out his disappointment and sorrow.

> *Is it nothing to you, all you who pass by? [he called out.]*
> *Look around and see.*
> *Is any suffering like my suffering*
> *that was inflicted on me,*
> *that the LORD brought on me*
> *in the day of his fierce anger?*
>
> *. . . My eyes overflow with tears.*
> *No one is near to comfort me,*
> *no one to restore my spirit.*

(Lamentations 1:12, 16)

But as with Job, right in the midst of his darkest day, Jeremiah inexplicably broke into a song of hope so beautiful, so profound, that it has shone in the darkness like a wide harvest moon for three thousand years.

> *Yet this I call to mind*
>> *and therefore I have hope:*
> *Because of the LORD'S great love we are not consumed,*
>> *for his compassions never fail.*
> *They are new every morning;*
>> *great is your faithfulness.*
> *I say to myself, "The LORD is my portion;*
>> *therefore I will wait for him."*
>
> *The LORD is good to those whose hope is in him,*
>> *to the one who seeks him;*
> *it is good to wait quietly*
>> *for the salvation of the LORD.*
>
> (Lamentations 3:21–26)

How many slump-shouldered travelers down through the long ages have warmed their hands and hearts at this fire? How many believers, through tears or with overpowering joy, have sung "Great Is Thy Faithfulness"? How many discouraged Christians have rolled out of bed in the morning and found a fresh supply of hope and strength for the day by quoting, "His compassions never fail. They are new every morning."

"His compassions never fail. They are new every morning."

It was just seventy-nine words (in English), but it became a ruby of wisdom and hope for Jeremiah — and millions upon countless millions of believers have held that ruby up to the light and found a double-handful of stick-with-it when they needed it most.

And here's just one more.

Saul of Tarsus, who became Paul the apostle, suffered like few others in the pages of the Bible. In his second letter to the church at Corinth, he felt it necessary to recount a few of those hardships. In the J. B. Phillips translation, it reads like this:

> I have worked harder than any of them. I have served more prison sentences! I have been beaten times without number. I have faced death again and again.
>
> I have been beaten the regulation thirty-nine stripes by the Jews five times.
>
> I have been beaten with rods three times. I have been stoned once. I have been shipwrecked three times. I have been twenty-four hours in the open sea.
>
> In my travels I have been in constant danger from rivers and floods, from bandits, from my own countrymen, and from pagans. I have faced danger in city streets, danger in the desert, danger on the high seas, danger among false Christians. I have known exhaustion, pain, long vigils, hunger and thirst, going without meals, cold and lack of clothing.
>
> Apart from all external trials I have the daily burden of responsibility for all the churches. Do you think anyone is weak without my feeling his weakness? Does anyone have his faith upset without my longing to restore him? (2 Corinthians 11:23–29 PHILLIPS)

In one particularly brutal incident, he was stoned by a mob, dragged out of town, and left for dead — or perhaps really did die for a few moments. He would later describe a time when he was "caught up to the third heaven ... caught up to paradise" (2 Corinthians 12:2–3). Could that have happened while he lay bleeding in the dust of Lystra? In those moments, he "heard inexpressible things, things that man is not permitted to tell" (2 Corinthians 12:4).

Paul was given a ruby of wisdom so rare, so sacred, so precious, that he kept it in secret for the rest of his days. Who knows what effect that vision had on his life? What we do know is that he went on to write thirteen books of the New Testament, giving believers of every generation, in numberless languages, a firm place to stand in a broken and uncertain world.

Solomon said that "wisdom is more precious than rubies, and *nothing you desire can compare with her*" (Proverbs 8:11 emphasis added).

Is that literally true? Will these rubies of wisdom be treasures we carry with us into eternity? Will they be insights with the capacity to change the course of lives, light dark places, and stoke the fires of weary ones on their last legs? Or do they have implications beyond this shadow-life, in the indescribable realities of the life to come?

In 1 Timothy 6:19, Paul speaks to his young friend about that safe-deposit box in heaven where our eternal riches are stored. He says, "In this way they will lay up treasure for themselves as a firm foundation for the coming age, so that they may take hold of the life that is truly life." In this particular context, of course, he is speaking of being rich in generosity, rich in good deeds. But note that this future-but-very-real wealth will provide some kind of added foundation, some incomprehensible eternal underpinning that will change something for us—something big—in the coming age.

Will these rubies of wisdom be like that?

The fact is, you acquire wisdom at the cost of long years. You gain wisdom at the price of obedience and perseverance. You buy wisdom with the currency of suffering in Christ.

If all these things are true—and I believe they are—then what I have endured in my wheelchair for over forty years was time well spent. And (I'm taking a deep breath here) *all* of the indignities, heartbreaking limitations, crushed hopes, days of sorrow, excruciating pain, and loss of so many simple joys of life rising out of my injury and paralysis have been worthwhile.

I can say to God, *"Thank You for this chair."*

Do I say that glibly? Do I make light of the suffering? Do I brush past the months of depression, frustration, disappointment, and sadness? If you take my word for anything, you must believe me that I do not. The apostle Paul could look back on his extreme hardships and call them "light and momentary troubles," and maybe one day I will look back and say the same thing.

But not yet. (More about that later.)

To this day my condition is difficult to bear—and perhaps even more so as my body bends and breaks down under the weight of four decades of paralysis.

But along the way, there have been rubies:

A sudden flash of insight, like a shaft of light piercing an overcast sky and illuminating—if only for a moment— a circle of darkened landscape.

Unheard-of opportunities to declare the name of Jesus in places where it has never been heard.

The inexpressible delight of bringing help and hope—and even a smile—to severely disabled people around the world who often feel forgotten by everyone, including God.

If there was ever such a thing as a time machine, I wish I could go back to that scared, angry, bitterly unhappy teenage girl named Joni Eareckson, hold a ruby to the light, and show her a little of what could come of her sorrow ... and her baby steps of faith.

But time moves on, and there is no going back.

So I share these few rubies with you.

———

In this you greatly rejoice, though now for a little while you may have had to suffer grief in all kinds of trials. These have come so that your faith—of greater worth than gold, which perishes even though refined by fire—may be proved genuine and may result in praise, glory and honor when Jesus Christ is revealed. (1 Peter 1:6–7)

1

The Anger That Heals

UNIVERSITY OF MARYLAND HOSPITAL,
BALTIMORE, MARYLAND,
NOVEMBER 1967

The surgery, they tell me, was a success. Something about bone chips, scraped from my hip, pressed like mortar in between the broken cervical vertebrae.

They say the graft—the patch job—is working well, and to celebrate, the doctor unscrewed the bolts in my head.

I'm out of ICU, free from the grip of the tongs, in a private room. Just like I wanted.

But what's changed? Nothing. My fingers ... where are they? My legs? My feet? Nothing moves from my neck down. If death has a taste—maybe something like dust, maybe something like ashes—it's on my tongue right now.

So here I am in my new room, staring at a high ceiling, listening to the drone of hospital sounds and nurses and orderlies padding softly down the corridor. The radiator under the high window makes a popping sound when the heat comes on. And somewhere there is a clock, endlessly ticking.

Today I counted the ceiling tiles. A hundred and forty, including partials. TV? It's too much work to watch from an angle like this. Isn't even worth the effort. I always heard people talk about time dragging. Busy and caught up with life as I was, I hardly knew what they meant.

I do now.

Hours. Days. Weeks. Months. Another season passing. Snow tinking softly against the window pane, piling up on the sill.

What's going on? Why am I not getting better?

And who am I talking to? God? A hidden camera in the ceiling?

This silence, it's choking me. My chest — so tight. *God, You can't do this!*

No. No! No tears ... not now. But here they come anyway. I can feel *those*. Welling up in my eyes, streaking across my face. And my nose running, with no way to blow it. Am I going crazy? How do you know if you're going insane? I've got to keep my mind occupied. I must do something ... think something.

This room ... swathed in white. Everything white. Crown molding, tiles, windows, walls. The doctors in their white lab coats, the nurses in their white uniforms, hose, caps, shoes. A world of white — but not real-world white, like the falling snow outside the window. This is antiseptic white. Sterile white. Laboratory white. Dead white. And here I am, Joni Eareckson, lying naked under a thin white sheet, waiting to be experimented on. I'm in the middle of a white, sterile box, stuck here by the force of gravity, drowning in a white darkness. Can't move. Can't feel. Just breathing and eating. That's it. That's life.

Do other people see themselves this way? Just existing? No ... they don't know it because they have too many things to distract them from the awful emptiness. They're busy doing stuff — holding down jobs, going to college, walking and running around.

But not me. No distractions here. I'm a guinea pig of a different color. Because I have nothing. *Do You hear, God? I have nothing to distract me. A big blank white zero! I don't even know if You're there. All I've got is a ceiling. A hundred and forty tiles. A hidden camera. The Eye in the sky.*

So what's it all about, God, or Ceiling, or whoever You are? Do You bring people into this world just to breathe, eat, grow old, and die? Do You toss the dice and paralyze people along the way? Or throw in a little cancer . . . a little Down syndrome . . . or maybe smash someone's brains in an accident? Well?

Tell me. . . . Why shouldn't I coerce one of my friends to bring me their father's razors or their mother's sleeping pills? Why not have the whole human race put a gun to its head, if we're just here to exist? Breathe in, breathe out. Exist. Is that all? IS THAT ALL?

Are You sadistic? Why do You leave me alive, God? Stop toying with me and just take me. I don't know what death is, but it can't be worse than this. . . . O God, I can't be this way, can't go on this way. How do I stop this long slide into nothingness?

But why should You even listen to me? If You were somewhere near me a few minutes ago—somewhere behind those ceiling tiles—now I have sent You away.

And even You can't see me, can't hear me. Or won't.

SOME FORTY YEARS LATER, AGOURA HILLS, CALIFORNIA

Joni, Joni.

So afraid. So alone. At the frayed end of her hope. What would I say to her, that lonely, despairing girl if I could be with her in that room, at her bedside?

Something in her knows her words are reckless. She's speaking to God like an Enemy. An Adversary. She wants to lash out and whip Him with her words. One scared little teenager, alone in a hospital room, still reeling from the horror of what her life has become.

She knows she needs God, needs Him like oxygen, yet imagines her words pushing Him even farther away. Should she have spoken like that, spitting those raw words into that antiseptic air, aiming every ounce of her anger and sorrow at a God who seemed to have retreated into an alternate universe, leaving her to suffer?

Yes.

And she is in good company … within the very pages of Scripture.

Another Slice of Life

Strange, isn't it, how the Bible itself captures such moments and enshrines them?

I'm reminded of that medical marvel of recent years called an EBT. Electron beam tomography is an ultra-sophisticated CAT scan able to capture images of bodily organs—especially the heart—that are in constant motion. The medical tech people will tell you that the EBT performs a complete, complex cycle of images with every heartbeat, producing them at one twentieth of a second. This allows doctors to look at the human heart, from top to bottom, in ultra-thin horizontal slices of both tissue and time.

That's what the Bible does too: it is "living and active. Sharper than any double-edged sword, it penetrates even to dividing soul and spirit, joints and marrow; it judges the thoughts and attitudes of the heart" (Hebrews 4:12).

Listen to this slice of a man's heart from the Psalms.

> *You have put me in the lowest pit,*
> *   in the darkest depths.*
> *Your wrath lies heavily upon me;*
> *   you have overwhelmed me with all your waves. . . .*
> *You have taken from me my closest friends*
> *   and have made me repulsive to them.*
> *I am confined and cannot escape;*
> *   my eyes are dim with grief.*
>
> (Psalm 88:6–7, 8–9)

There it is, a membrane-thin cutting of a human soul. Hold it to the light and you can see right through it, like India paper.

Who said such words? It's attributed to someone named "Heman the Ezrahite," in Psalm 88. Who was he, and why did his cry in the night find its way into a book that would endure until the end of time and on into eternity?

The writer goes on:

> *Why, O LORD, do you reject me*
> *and hide your face from me?*
>
> *From my youth I have been afflicted and close to death;*
> *I have suffered your terrors and am in despair.*
> *Your wrath has swept over me;*
> *your terrors have destroyed me.*
> *All day long they surround me like a flood;*
> *they have completely engulfed me.*
>
> (Psalm 88:14–17)

You won't likely see this psalm on a poster populated with summer daisies. This is a raw cry of despair, with serrated edges. And this frightened, lonely man, an anonymous nobody named Heman the Ezrahite, weeps his words to a seemingly unresponsive heaven.

This is no sweet psalm of David, wrapping up with a step-back, heavenly perspective and a fireworks finale of praise. Heman ends his psalm with a sob, a cry trailing into the night.

> *You have taken my companions and loved ones from me;*
> *the darkness is my closest friend.*
>
> (v. 18)

End of psalm. End of story. Close the book. Fade to black. *Darkness is my closest friend.*

What do you think? Does that speak well of the Lord? There seems to be no attempt to leave readers with a warm, cozy impression of God-my-refuge. It simply ends, leaving you hanging suspended in the void, isolated in some nameless dungeon of fear, confusion, and grief.

It's an EBT slice of a soul. And the eternal God, whose eye misses nothing, took this image of Heman the Ezrahite's despair and put it on the screen.

For the ages.

Why did He do that? Because broken-hearted Heman's slice of life may well be just like ours. If God took one twentieth of a second images of our soul and threw them on a monitor, some of those paper-thin instants in time would look very much like the soul sample of this desolate psalmist.

The Joni of long ago, the Joni that was me, imagined that her harsh words against God would push her even farther away from Him—which she thought she wanted but really didn't want at all. And of course God knew that.

One of the first places I turned after my accident was to the book of Job. As I lay immobilized in the hospital, my mind swirled with questions. When I learned that my paralysis was permanent, it raised even more questions.

Do you have any concept of how desperate I was to find answers?

Job, I reasoned, had suffered terribly and questioned God again and again. And make no mistake, Job's questions weren't of the polite Wednesday-night-Bible-study variety. They were pointed, sharp, and seemed at times to walk the borderline of blasphemy.

Why didn't You let me die at birth? (3:11)

Why didn't You dry up my mother's breasts so that I would starve? (3:12)

Why do You keep wretched people like me alive? (3:20–22)

Do You really expect me to have hope and patience? (6:11)

What do You think I'm made of, anyway? Stone? Metal? (6:12)

If life is so short, does it have to be miserable too? (7:1–10)

Why don't You just back off and stop hurting me for awhile? (7:17, 19)

What did I ever do to You that I became target practice for
   Your arrows? (7:20)

Why don't You forgive me before I die and it's too late? (7:21)

Why do You always favor the bad guys? (9:24)

Since You've already decided I'm guilty, why should I even try?
   (9:29)

You're the One who created me, so why are You destroying
   me? Does that make sense? (10:8)

Why don't You let me meet You somewhere face to face so I
   can state my case? (23:3–6)

Job's friends were aghast. They half expected lightning to fall
and fry the suffering man for such impudence. But no lightning fell.
In fact, God greatly preferred the honest, gut-wrenching cries of Job
to the self-righteous prattle of the so-called comforters who mouthed
all the old formulas and traditional bromides.

What meant the most to me in my suffering was that God never
condemned Job for his doubt and despair. God seemed ready and
willing to take on the hardball questions. Ah, but the answers?
They weren't quite the ones Job had expected.

Likewise, when it comes right down to it, I'm not sure if it would
have sufficed to find "the answers" to all of my questions anyway.
Could I have even begun to handle it? It would have been like down-
loading the entire contents of the Internet onto an old laptop com-
puter. It would have been like pouring million-gallon truths into a
Dixie cup. My poor pea-brain wouldn't have been able to process it.

For some odd reason, however, it comforted me to realize that
God did not condemn me for plying Him with questions. He wanted
me to express the true contents of my heart, to dump out all the
jumbled, jagged shards of my soul before Him.

Sometimes we're afraid to talk to God this way — like Job crying
out in the night on the ash heap behind his house, like the psalmist
treading water in the dark, like a furious teenager welded into bed

with a broken neck and bolts in her head. We repress those murky, edgy emotions about our suffering. We choose to be polite, speaking sanitized words, or not speaking at all. We bottle up our troubling questions and unspeakable feelings toward God, hiding behind an orthodox, evangelical glaze as we "give it all over to the Lord."

Except that we don't. It's a lie and a ruse.

And He knows that too.

Why would God rather have our anger, our venom, our rage, our cry of desolation rather than our measured, controlled, even-tempered, theologically correct prayer?

It's all about the heart. Over and over again in Scripture you can hear God saying, "Give Me your heart or nothing at all."

God doesn't have time to play games. He wants reality.

In the book of Malachi, God responds to the bored, perfunctory worship of Israel's priests, going through a cynical litany of religious motions. God said, "Oh, that one of you would shut the temple doors, so that you would not light useless fires on my altar! I am not pleased with you ... and I will accept no offering from your hands" (Malachi 1:10).

The Lord is saying, "Why even pretend? Don't bother! If you don't really believe in what you're doing, if it doesn't engage you to the very soul, then padlock the temple doors, nail plywood over the windows, and walk away. I would rather that you did!"

In the New Testament, Jesus didn't need an EBT unit to sample the soul tissue of the Pharisees. He told them: "Isaiah was right when he prophesied about you hypocrites; as it is written: 'These people honor me with their lips, but their hearts are far from me. They worship me in vain'" (Mark 7:6–7).

In other words, they talked the talk, but it had nothing— nothing whatsoever—to do with the real content of their hearts. When they "prayed," they weren't really speaking to God at all. They were *scripted*, mouthing all the expected words at all the anticipated times.

And it made Jesus sick.

Contrast that with another slice of soul, late in the gospel of Luke. On the Lord's final approach to Jerusalem, on His way to fulfill the driving mission that brought Him to earth and gave Him human flesh, on His way past Jericho, He heard a scream from the back of the crowd.

No measured tones here. No well-considered, finely modulated words. Just a dry, raspy yell from the back of the crowd. An anguished cry for help.

"Jesus, Son of David, have mercy on me!"

And it stopped the Son of God in mid-stride. He had the blind man brought forward. I can picture Him laying a hand on the man's trembling, rounded shoulder and saying, "What do you want me to do for you?" (See Luke 18:35 – 43.)

Front Burner

What do we do when we repress our disappointment and anger before the Lord? All we've done is shove the problem to the back burner. There it simmers. This is *real* trouble. We can't smell problems burning when they're repressed. And so we naively think "things will work out." But they don't. Hope is aroused, then deferred. It revives, then gets snuffed out again. "Hope deferred makes the heart sick" (Proverbs 13:12).

Then the fire goes out and our hearts become stone cold.

Anger keeps pushing the problem to the front burner. Fiery feelings keep the problem a hot potato, bouncing from hand to hand, propelling us into action and triggering activity. We aren't allowed to wallow in our failures. Hot-hearted rage spurs an immediate and decisive choice and forces us to face our need.

Anger — even the sort of cynical, furious emotions the Joni of 1967 experienced in the shock and revulsion of her circumstances — may not be all that bad. When Ephesians 4:26 says, "In your anger do not sin," it's clear that hostility is not always synonymous with sin. Not all anger is wrong.

Cancer, bankruptcy, divorce, betrayal, or the birth of longed-for children with multiple handicaps push people to extremes. And please hear me here: Affliction will either *warm you up* toward spiritual things or *turn you cold*. Jesus said in Revelation 3:15–16: "I know your deeds, that you are neither cold nor hot. I wish you were either one or the other! So, because you are lukewarm—neither hot nor cold—I am about to spit you out of my mouth."

Hate is sometimes closer to love than a temperate, smiling indifference. And lukewarmness is the only road that never gets to God. There's nothing mediocre, tepid, or halfway about feelings of fury.

Strong emotions open the door to asking really hard questions—and I asked so very many of them in the early days of my paralysis. Does life make sense? Is God good? More to the point, our deep emotions reveal the spiritual direction in which we are moving. Are we moving toward the Almighty or away from Him? Anger properly makes *Someone* the issue of our suffering rather than some *thing*. And that's moving in the right direction.

The newly paralyzed Joni, for all her seething rage at the God-behind-the-ceiling-tiles, was aiming those emotions at *Him*. Whether she understood it at the time or not, she was moving toward Him in her despair, venting her disappointment, expressing hurt, and even questioning His goodness. But she wasn't talking about God behind God's back. She was angry enough to engage Him head-on. And then the anger melted into tears, and she was a scared little girl again, calling out to a daddy she couldn't see.

God, I can't . . . I can't live like this. If You won't let me die, then please show me how to live.

It wasn't exactly a ringing prayer of faith. But it left the door open for Him to respond. And He would. Because "the LORD is close to the brokenhearted and saves those who are crushed in spirit" (Psalm 34:18). Do we really believe that?

The word translated "crushed" in this verse comes from a Hebrew root that means "to burst." It can also be translated "to tear," as in tearing a piece of cloth down the middle. When you are in so much pain, sorrow, or frustration that it feels as though your heart might burst within you, when you feel like your soul has been torn like rotten fabric, God draws close to help. You don't even have to dial 911 or push that little blue On-Star button. He's there with you instantly, ready to hear and respond to your cries of perplexity and anguish.

Sometimes brokenhearted people say harsh things. Sometimes some toxic cynicism or long-repressed anger can spurt out of a lacerated heart. The Lord knows that ... and wants to be close anyway. Sometimes bitter emotions and acid words can ooze from a crushed spirit. The Lord understands that, as well ... and draws near to comfort.

The fact is, gut-wrenching questions honor God. Despair directed at His throne is a way of encountering Him, opening ourselves up to the one and only Someone who can actually do something about our plight. And whether we collide head-on with Him or simply bump up against Him in the dark, we cannot be the same.

We never are when we experience God.

Airing Our Complaints

Most of the time, of course, we can manage.

Like jugglers spinning plates on long sticks. And if we get unfairly reprimanded at work or a ticket for speeding, we squeeze in a heart-to-heart talk with a close friend before rushing to spin the next plate. We keep a journal, venting our frustrations on paper. We soak in the tub, sweat on the treadmill, splurge on a new dress, or get away to the mountains for a weekend. Prayer groups and Bible studies help. God won't load us up with more plates than we can handle and, with His enabling, we will be able to keep them spinning.

But sometimes we're hard pressed to believe it.

Something, we assume, has to give.

When pain lumbers through the front door, squats down in the middle of our lives, and makes itself at home day after day, year after year, we can choke. Crack. Erupt in anger.

God is big enough to take on anger like this. He is not flustered.

First, He knows stuff happens. He Himself said, "In this world you will have trouble" (John 16:33). Second, He doesn't tiptoe around it, embarrassed and at wit's end to explain our woes. He doesn't cover up the gore and guts of a person's rage, like a Mafia hit man who trashes his blood-stained gloves so he doesn't get nailed.

Remember, God's rage nailed God. He wrote the book on suffering. And He invited people like Job, Jeremiah, and the author of Psalm 88 to be his coauthors. In so doing, He opens the doors for His disappointed, sometimes-angry sons and daughters to air their complaints.

Take your grievances directly to the Lord, which means moving toward the Lord. Go ahead and vent disappointment, express hurt, and even question the goodness of the Almighty. But whatever you do, don't badmouth Him to others. Please don't sow seeds of discord or incite rebellion among friends against God. Don't talk behind His back. Engage Him, head on.

When you think about it, the people you really get angry with are the ones you trust most deeply. To say, "I am mad as a hornet, God, and I don't understand what you are doing one bit!" sounds like the dark side of trust, but it is trust nonetheless.

Good Reason to Be Angry?

Speaking of angry servants of God, I've always been fascinated by God's conversation with the prophet Jonah.

After Jonah had gone to some pains (to say the least) to bring a stern word of judgment to the hated Assyrians in Nineveh, he was thoroughly disgusted to see that the message actually hit home. The choir sang "Just As I Am," and the whole evil city came forward in repentance—from the king on the throne to the little guy shining sandals on the sidewalk.

It was the most dramatic change of heart ever recorded.

Imagine a Billy Graham crusade in New York City where *everyone* received Christ. The mayor, the police department, the Yankees, the garbage collectors, the prostitutes, and the editorial board of the *New York Times*—everyone.

What evangelist wouldn't give anything for a harvest like that?

Well, there was one. And it happened to be the preacher at the Great Nineveh Crusade, Jonah himself.

> But it greatly displeased Jonah and he became angry. He prayed to the LORD and said, "Please LORD, was not this what I said while I was still in my own country? Therefore in order to forestall this I fled to Tarshish, for I knew that You are a gracious and compassionate God, slow to anger and abundant in lovingkindness, and one who relents concerning calamity. Therefore now, O LORD, please take my life from me, for death is better to me than life."
>
> The LORD said, "Do you have good reason to be angry?" (Jonah 4:1–4 NASB)

Jonah was so angry he wanted to die. As a loyal Israelite, he hated these smug Assyrians in their capital of cruelty. They were the militant Islamic fascists of his day. They had threatened and bullied and afflicted Israel for generations, and there was no more evil, sadistic, blood-thirsty people on the planet. And now they ask for forgiveness and God says, "Yes."

Just like that.

It infuriated the prophet. He said in essence, "I knew it. Knew it! You asked me to preach to this God-forsaken evil empire and instead of blowing You off, they suddenly get serious about God. And now You're going to let them all off the hook just because You're so merciful and kind. It disgusts me! If this is the way Your world runs, then I want to get off at the next stop."

Maybe Jonah thought his own words were so out of line that God would just incinerate him on the spot. But He didn't. Instead, He reasoned with His servant.

"Do you have good reason to be angry?"

The Almighty God of the universe reasoning with one angry man? Does that make sense? Wouldn't it be like a man taking time to reason with a two-year-old? Or a cat? Or an ant?

God was saying, in effect, "Cool down a minute, Son. Let's talk about this. You're angry, but why should you be?"

Jonah was so upset he didn't even reply. He went out to a high spot on the east of the great city and tried to find a little shade while he watched things unfold. The Bible says God caused a leafy vine to shade the prophet from the scorching heat, and the prophet "was extremely happy about the plant." But then the Lord sent a worm, which attacked the plant overnight so that it withered—leaving Jonah exposed to the sun again.

Again, the prophet was furious with God, and God came back to reason with him just a little bit more.

> Then God said to Jonah, "Do you have good reason to be angry about the plant?" And he said, "I have good reason to be angry, even to death." Then the LORD said, "You had compassion on the plant for which you did not work and which you did not cause to grow, which came up overnight and perished overnight. Should I not have compassion on Nineveh, the great city in which there are more than 120,000 persons who do not know the difference between their right and left hand, as well as many animals?" (Jonah 4:9–10 NASB)

Instead of rebuking Jonah for his anger, God conversed with

him. He dialogued. He gave his servant a little object lesson. Then He said, "That's not just a city, Jonah. There are thousands of people behind those walls. Babies in bassinets. Toddlers playing in front of their houses. Young people who haven't made up their minds about the evil culture they were born into. Not to mention all the animals who have never harmed anyone. And look at that king. Evil as he has been, when he heard the truth, he *responded*. He humbled himself. Even the kings of Israel haven't been willing to do that. Do you see him? He's leading his people in a national revival. And you still want to kill them all? Is that reasonable, Jonah?"

That's where the book ended, and since the author was most likely Jonah himself, we can assume that the prophet reflected on this conversation over the months and years of his life, and came around to God's point of view.

As childish and petulant as Jonah's anger at God may seem to us, it was the best thing that could have happened to him because it brought the issues of his heart out into the light of day. Instead of running *from* God, he began talking *to* God. And he found that God was not only willing to listen; He was ready to dialogue about the issue at hand.

The Dark Side

There is, however, a dark side to anger, and Jonah came perilously close to the danger zone. The danger wasn't that God would slap him down for arguing. The danger was anger turned inward to the point that the prophet — twice — wanted to end his life.

Uncontrolled anger has incredible potential to destroy. It digresses into a black energy that demands immediate release and relief. It despises being vulnerable and helpless. It relishes staying in control. It loathes dependence on God and so gains macabre pleasure in spreading the poison of mistrust. Ironically, this sort of anger—unrighteous anger—turns on us. It is a liar, offering us satisfaction, when in truth, it guts us and leaves us empty.

Who can endure such emptiness?

Unrighteous anger—anger that leads us away from God—sucks the last vestige of hope from our hearts. We stop caring, stop feeling. We commit a silent suicide of the soul, and sullen despair moves in like a terrible damp fog, deadening our heart to the hope that we will ever be rescued, redeemed, and happy again.

God will not stand for this.

He is intolerant of despair.

He will not permit our puny shields of unrighteous anger to stall Him. And so He encroaches, presumes, invades, and infringes. He tears aside the curtains of despondency and throws open locked doors. He hits the light switch in our dark hearts. He pierces our complacency and boldly intrudes into our self-pity, brashly calling it what it is and challenging us to leave it behind.

He does it, occasionally, by heaping on trouble.

I'll never forget when God crashed through my despair.

Somewhere after the first year of lying paralyzed in my hospital bed, somewhere after my bleak prognosis drained every ounce of hope—even anger, righteous and unrighteous—out of me, despair moved in. I refused to get up for physical therapy. I turned my head away when friends came to visit.

Hazel, a black nurse's aide from Mississippi, noticed I was slipping away. She knew I had taken a liking to her. Ambling into my room, she would pull up a chair, and take her cigarette breaks by my bed.

"Wanna tell me about it, girl?" she'd ask, lighting up.

No reply.

She would smile, slowly blowing a stream of smoke in the other direction.

I'd grunt.

"You feel like bawling," she'd say, "you just tell me." She patted her pocket. "I've got a kerchief here handy."

"Um." I was numb. I didn't want to talk.

I didn't want to eat. Once when Hazel was feeding me dinner, half-chewed food dribbled out of the side of my mouth. "What in the world are you doing?" she shouted. My body reacted with a violent spasm. Hazel slammed down the fork and peas scattered.

Picking up a napkin, she forcefully wiped my mouth, crumpled it, and threw it down on the tray. "You get yourself together, girl. Ain't nothing wrong with you that a good look around this hospital won't cure."

My cheeks flushed with embarrassment. I fought back tears.

"Now are you gonna eat this or what?"

Hazel had roused deep feelings of resentment. My eyes narrowed. "Yes," I spat back. The food was tasteless and hard. I chewed mechanically, forcing myself to swallow against a knotted stomach. Not a word was spoken between us. After she left, I struggled harder to contain the tears. I could not allow myself to cry because there would be no one to blow my nose or change my damp pillow.

Suddenly a realization shot across my mind.

I'm feeling something.

Like a hibernating animal waking up, I felt something stir. No more emotional numbness. Instead, a magnetic pull toward hope. In the darkness, I found myself whispering to God, pleading for His mercy and help.

My prayer was short, hardly more than a word or two, but it left the door open for Him to respond. Little did I realize that He would.

In the next few days, I sensed a stronger interest in the Bible. When I lay face down on the Stryker frame, I was able to flip the pages of a Bible with my mouth stick. I didn't know where to turn, but the psalms drew me — and Job.

And in those two books in the middle of my Bible, I encountered other heartbroken people with hard questions for the Almighty.

The damp fog of my despair did not dissipate overnight, but I knew beyond all doubt I had turned a corner. I was moving in the direction of God. My questions had also created a paradox: In the midst of God's absence, I felt His presence. I found Him after I let go of what I thought He *should* be or do. My despair ended up being my ally, because through it, He took hold of me.

And I would say this to that Joni of long ago: "Your cry in the dark is better, Joni, than turning your face to the wall and sealing God out. At least you spoke to Him. At least you called out. At least you hurled those emotions of fear mingled with hate toward God Himself. And you drew the very attention of heaven."

He has loved you and kept you through all your days.

Scripture calls every one of us to the throne of grace, but doesn't tell us how to get there. Maybe it doesn't matter. Run, walk, or crawl on your stomach through the muck. Come in your tears, come in your rage, come in your perplexity, come in your anguish of soul. Just come, and mercy awaits you.

So now, "forty years of life in a wheelchair" later, here is the ruby, hard-won. Here is the wisdom I would so love to give my younger self. You're on the right track, Joni. You're facing the right direction. Tell God what's in your heart ... all of it. Then settle back, if only for a moment, in the memory of who He has been to you, and how He has loved you and kept you through all your days.

Reasoning with God

When tragedy blindsides you and almost knocks you silly, you are understandably bewildered. You feel confusion and panic. You may feel afraid that more hardship will come on top of it all. In your anger and fear, you may feel like cursing, or retreating into depression and despair. You may feel a thousand things. But at some point, somewhere along the line, if you don't stop *feeling* and start *thinking* about how to attend the circumstances in which you find yourself, you will freeze.

Your mind will go into lockdown, and it will be difficult for anyone to break through to you ... even God.

Yes, intense suffering calls for deep emotions. In the aftermath of a terrible tragedy, people weep. We *should* weep. God weeps. But there is also a time to think. And neither can replace the other.

When you are able to raise your head above the heartache in which you are swimming, the Bible tells you to take the next step. It is full of commands to "think," "ponder," "consider," "weigh," and "judge." Again, remember how God addressed His servant Jonah when the man was smoldering with anger? He said, "Doest thou well to be angry?" (Jonah 4:4 KJV). In other words, "Think about this, son. Are you being reasonable? Is it right for you to respond this way?"

Jesus often turned questions about the meaning of life, death, and suffering back onto the questioner. "What is written in the Law?" He would ask. Expecting an argument, people would blink, sniff back their feelings, flip the pages in their mind, think out loud, and come up with relevant passages. But this didn't end the discussion. Next was the real work. "How do you read it?" He would ask. In other words, "What do you think these Scriptures mean?"

He reasoned with them.

He invited their participation.

He challenged them to think things through.

He encouraged them to let the real truths of Scripture break through the crust of their brittle preconceptions and rigid prejudices.

What you think about God influences your friendship with Him. It affects how much glory you give to Him. The King James translation of Proverbs 23:7 may not be the best rendering we have of those words, but the thought remains true: "For as he thinketh in his heart, so is he."

Please hear these next words. They have come to me as a ruby, hard-won through the years: Your imagination about God — *especially* in the midst of tragedy — isn't reliable. We must run to the true portrait He gives us in His Word.

If we simply trust our emotions about Him, we re-create Him in our own image ... as I did when I thought of Him as "The Big Camera Eye in the Ceiling." Deep down I didn't really believe that about God, but the more I let that thought bounce through the despair-twisted corridors of my emotions, the more it became "real" to me.

Your imagination about God — especially in the midst of tragedy — isn't reliable.

Our best source of information about who God is — no matter how we might happen to feel about it on any given moment — comes right off the pages of Scripture. We must cling to those truths — digging in our fingernails — as we would cling to a rock in a fast-rushing stream.

If our surging emotions cause us to hold more tightly to His Word (for dear life), then they have swept us in a good direction.

Breathing Room

Last night, the nightmare came in person.

It was after the lights were out. Was it a hallucination from all these heavy drugs they're pumping into me? A demon? I don't know, I don't care. I just know it tried to kill me. It slipped into the room (I could hear its hooves clicking on the linoleum), and placed a large concrete block on my chest, crushing me. *I couldn't breathe.* I started screaming and a nurse rushed in. "Get it off! Please, get it *off!*"

"Joni," she said, "it's only your hands on your chest. That's all. Your hands were crossed on top of your abdomen. You're okay. You're *okay.*"

Easy for her to say. Maybe next time, she'll be too late. Maybe next time that thing will smother me.

FORTY YEARS LATER

At the best of times, quadriplegia is confinement.

At the worst of times, it is near suffocation.

Claustrophobia is an adversary I've had to deal with since those earliest days in ICU after my accident, strapped in upside down and so tight to my metal and canvas Stryker frame that all I could move was my head—slightly. In one terrifying episode a few days after my accident, right after they had flipped me facedown on my Stryker frame, I lost all ability to breathe at all and had to be resuscitated.

Yes, sometimes the reasons for the claustrophobia are physical.

Just recently, in the hospital for nine days with double pneumonia, my old enemy rose up with a vengeance. Try to imagine lying flat and not being able to raise your head and cough when you feel that tightness and gurgling in your bronchial area. Imagine not being able to sit up in bed or at least raise up on your elbows. Sometimes it's like an invisible hand pressing an invisible pillow over your face.

It's worse at night. It always is.

Thankfully, Ken put two chairs together and slept by my bed, so I could at least quiet my heart knowing someone was there to help sit me up every time I needed to expel phlegm.

But claustrophobia isn't always about congested lungs or oxygen deprivation. Sometimes the circumstances of life hedge us in so tightly, restrict us so severely, press us so relentlessly, that we feel like we're being crushed.

Back in 1980, I came back home to the family farm after making the movie *Joni*. It was an especially difficult season in my life. I was extremely thin, emotionally exhausted, and still brooding over some of the movie scenes we'd just filmed. Reliving those horrific days of my injury and the early years of my paralysis brought some troubling feelings to the surface of my heart—issues I thought I'd resolved years before.

One evening I was in bed watching an old movie on TV, *The Bird Man of Alcatraz*. In one of the scenes, Burt Lancaster releases one of his birds through the bars of his cell, watching it take wing and soar into the wide blue sky. Suddenly the expression on his face turns from a look of pleasure and affection for the little bird to one of sheer horror. As the bird takes to the skies, the terrible reality of his fate suddenly dawns on the prisoner. *The bird is free, but you'll never be free. Your circumstances will never change. You'll always, always be confined. Until you die.*

Just that quickly the walls of the farmhouse bedroom closed in on me, and I panicked, screaming at my sister to turn off the movie. I couldn't get my breath, and she had to sit me up in bed and press on my abdomen to help me to breathe. I had never felt so claustrophobic. I had never experienced the circumstances of my life binding me like that, squeezing the air right out of the room.

Although the Lord has granted me more mobility since those earliest days — including more maneuverable power wheelchairs and driving my own van on the California freeways — I have never escaped that recurring feeling of the walls drawing together around me, shrinking the room, constricting and asphyxiating me.

But I'm not the only one.

Hedged In

I come back to Job again. Here was a man (who better?) who knew what it meant to have the walls of grief and desolation press in on him, pushing him to the edge of sanity. As with that younger Joni in the Baltimore hospital so long ago, the long nights brought him terror and dread rather than sleep and rest:

> When I think my bed will comfort me
>   and my couch will ease my complaint,
> even then you frighten me with dreams
>   and terrify me with visions,
> so that I prefer strangling and death,
>   rather than this body of mine.
>   (Job 7:13–15)

Sometimes our life circumstances leave us feeling like we have

nowhere to turn. We can stay inside or go outside, we can drive to
the mall or out into the desert—but it doesn't matter, because our
grief comes with us. Feeling himself wrapped with heaviness to the
point of asphyxiation, the patriarch wrote:

> *Why is life given to a man*
> *whose way is hidden,*
> *whom God has hedged in?*
> (Job 3:23)

Hedged in.

Pressed into a space so constricting that you feel like you can't
even get your breath. Have you been there?

The four walls of a sick room can feel terribly confining, even if
you are only in bed for a short time. When I was stuck in a hospital
room for over a year, those walls felt like a jail. I resonated with the
prophet who wrote, "He has walled me in so I cannot escape; he has
weighed me down with chains" (Lamentations 3:7).

There is a lot of lament in that verse.

But there is also comfort. Do you see it?

Who was the stone mason who walled Jeremiah in? Whose hedge
and whose walls are we speaking about here? This is *God's* hedge.
Those are *God's* walls. The prophet didn't understand his situation,
but he knew Who had placed him there. Job acknowledged that it
wasn't bad luck or random circumstances that had hedged him in; it
was God Himself . . . though in his sorrow he couldn't imagine why.

That thought comforts me now, but I'm not sure it would
have comforted me in the early days of my injury. I would have
thought God was a sadist or simply didn't care about little Joni in
Maryland.

But now, forty years into my quadriplegia, I am at peace with the
ways and walls of a sovereign God. He has hedged me in and put me
where I am. He has *placed* me, not misplaced me. He knows exactly
where I am and how to care for me.

Here is a ruby, hard-won. If you find yourself in a confining situation, it is God who has confined you. He is the One who has surrounded you and hemmed you in. It is only when we view our restricting circumstances as being placed there by God's hand that we find courage to face, accept, and even embrace the wall and the hedge.

If you find yourself in a confining situation, it is God who has confined you.

Walls are cold, hard, and foreboding. Robert Frost wrote, "Something there is that doesn't love a wall." And hedges? They are dense, unyielding, and thorny. But the love of your God is supreme and matchless, and He only confines you for a wise and timely purpose. For those who believe in the love and the wisdom of a sovereign God, even a heartbreaking confinement can be a place of building trust.

In fact, it may become the widest place you have ever experienced.

Hard-Pressed

"We are hard-pressed on every side, but not crushed" (2 Corinthians 4:8).

The apostle Paul was another prominent member of the Boxed-In Club. "I'm hard-pressed," he told the Corinthians.

When you and I say something like that, we might mean we have a term paper deadline coming up, a cluster of nagging household tasks to attend to, or maybe even some health issues or legal problems that trouble us. But when Paul said "hard-pressed," he wasn't using the term lightly. It wasn't as though he was saying, "Whew, we were really up against it there for awhile."

A few pages earlier in the same letter, Paul described circumstances so oppressive and pressure so intense that it was "far beyond our ability to endure, so that we despaired even of life" (2 Corinthians

1:8). He actually teetered on the edge of giving up. The pressure was *that* bad.

What kinds of pressures? We're not told. Probably a baker's dozen of serious, critical issues layered one on top of another. Legal pressures. Financial pressures. Health pressures. Relationship pressures. Spiritual warfare pressures. Paul had to deal with slander, lies, emotional stress, loneliness, betrayal, threats, physical abuse, a failing body, plots on his life, and fierce — even Satanic — opposition wherever he turned.

In the King James Version, Paul says he was "pressed out of measure, above strength" (2 Corinthians 1:8). Why? It doesn't really matter. He wanted this rich, sophisticated, urban church in Corinth to taste a small slice of his life, to understand that their apostle had been so burdened that he actually thought he wouldn't live through it.

Yet in the very same letter, Paul could say, "We are hard-pressed on every side, yet *not crushed*" (2 Corinthians 4:8, emphasis added). That last word ... *crushed*. In the original language, it literally means "cramped" or "hemmed in."

But how could that be? What did he mean? How can you be encircled, pressed in, and hedged about and *not* be cramped? How can you be confined, shackled, chained, locked in, and closed up in a dungeon and *not* be hemmed in? How can you live large in a confined area with strict limitations?

The fact is, a high hedge cannot shut out our view of the skies, nor can it prevent the soul from looking up into the face of God. That's what happened to me in the hospital during that long, long year of confinement. As the days and weeks went by, I earnestly wrestled with God, pleading and praying to Him. "O LORD; in the morning will I direct my prayer unto thee, and will *look up*" (Psalm 5:3 KJV, italics mine).

Looking back, it was dreadfully difficult. Yet in another sense, I experienced *more* freedom than I had ever known. It was yet another of those inexplicable ironies in the kingdom of God. Yes, there were stretches of boredom, frustration, tears, and sadness of heart. But it was also a rich and deeply spiritual time which I wouldn't trade for anything. Because there is so little else to see, the hedged-in Christian cannot afford to hang his head. He must look up. And it is *that* Christian who may possibly apprehend God more fully than the disciple who moves about freely and unconfined.

I have a friend who went through deep waters several years ago. He described the weeks and months that followed as the darkest days of his life. Feeling as though he was drowning in depression and grief, he sought the Lord with a desperation beyond anything he had ever experienced. As a result, he learned a new way to pray in those days—on his face on the living room carpet, arms outstretched, as dependent as a little child.

Looking back on those days, my friend recalls how narrow his world had become, with the suffocating darkness pressing in from all sides. His Bible became as thin as a half dozen of his favorite psalms. But he also remembers an indescribable connection with God, as if a larger channel had been opened between them. It resulted in a new sense of God's presence and an ability to discern His voice. His new standard for prayer was his nose buried in the carpet fibers, his arms out in front of him, palms up. He learned that the lower he placed himself before God, the more he expressed his utter dependence on the Lord for everything, the sooner God's miraculous work of healing and restoration began in his life.

Hard-pressed and hedged in? Just remember that where the Spirit of the Lord is ... *wherever* the Spirit of the Lord is, there is freedom. And hope. And light. And even beauty.

Responsible for My Response

Paul may not have been responsible for the circumstances that so totally overwhelmed him, but he was responsible for the way he responded to those circumstances. And how did he respond? He didn't groan, "Oh, for Pete's sake, here we go again." Instead, he said, "For Christ's sake, I delight in weaknesses.... For when I am weak, then I am strong" (2 Corinthians 12:10).

I like that.

It's for Christ's sake. His glory. For His good name and reputation.

Paul wasn't fixated on his chains; he was focused on his Savior.

Consider the incident in Philippi described in Acts 16. The magistrates handcuffed Paul and Silas to a scourging pole and gave them a brutal whipping. Piling humiliation upon humiliation, the Philippian authorities then took the bruised and lacerated missionaries and placed them in stocks in an inner cell of the city jail.

There they were, stuck in a wet, stinky dungeon tucked away from the light of day. Paul must have been faint. Silas must have been sick to his stomach. Every bone ached and their fresh wounds oozed.

Yet deep in that dark, confining place, walled in by stone, secured in stocks and chains, they do the incredible. At midnight, the darkest and loneliest hour, they began praying and singing praises to God. They weren't just humming along lightly or mumbling their prayers between moans and groans. No, this must have been a loud, rich, two-part harmony. In spite of the thick walls and heavy doors, Luke says that the other prisoners "were listening to them."

Their words — those improbable songs of praise rising out of the most severe confinement — won the battle against Satan in that midnight hour. As it says in Psalm 106:47:

> *Save us, O LORD our God,*
> *and gather us . . .*
> *that we may give thanks to your holy name*
> *and glory in your praise.*

To whine or grumble, fret or murmur, complain or lament, would have been to invite defeat in that terrible hour. And who would have blamed Paul and Silas if they had sputtered a nasty remark or two?

But the record shows that they didn't. They didn't succumb in defeat with thoughtless, ill-tempered words. They triumphed in a victory of praise. What a witness to the other prisoners! What a testimony to the jailer. And what an encouragement to countless generations of oppressed believers who have read that account and reached back for a second wind.

We *are* responsible. Maybe we're not accountable for some of our trials, but we are accountable for all of our responses. If Paul and Silas could sing choruses in a dungeon, you and I can offer praise *wherever* life places us. This very moment.

This isn't to minimize the suffering, or the suffocating feelings of those who find themselves cornered, confined, and pressed in by anguish, physical limitations, or even the literal walls of a prison. Listen, I'm a quadriplegic. I *understand.* My heart especially aches for people who suffer with chronic physical pain. Oh, how hope is needed!

The Narrow Walls of Pain

My friend Christy has multiple sclerosis *and* diabetes. If you know anything about those conditions, you know that this woman deals with ceaseless pain. You can see it in her eyes. What I like about Christy is that she isn't about to be beaten to a pulp by this double-whammy of a medical condition. She has started a support group to help other Christians who wrestle with pain, and she also writes a regular column for the encouragement of others.

That's all well and good, but because she's taken charge—stepped into a role of spokeswoman and leader—many onlookers see her as a spiritual giant. How does she respond to that? In one of her recent columns she wrote: "People assume that no matter what happens, you'll face it with the faith of Noah, the patience of Job, and the courage of David. That is a fine goal to be sure, but more often I find myself reacting like Peter … sinking and crying out, 'Lord, save me!'"

Bless her for saying that! You may not have MS or diabetes, you may not be a quadriplegic like me, but you definitely have days when you feel like you're sinking, drowning, going down for the third time. Try as you will, you simply can't meet everyone's expectations. Bills pile up, checkbooks don't balance, you were too late to file an extension on your taxes, the store won't take back your return item without a receipt, and then the proverbial straw that broke the camel's back, the checkout clerk forgot to bag your eggs—the main thing that took you to the store to begin with!

Small things. Almost silly things. But when you are already hedged-in, hard-pressed, and maxed-out trying to deal with nonstop pain, you begin to feel like you're drowning. Like Peter, you're sinking in the stormy waves, and you cry out, "Lord, save me!"

And then there are those times when pain seems to take over everything. Another friend, Michael, wrote to me:

> *Two years ago, tumors were pinching my sciatic nerve and I was forced to my knees in tears. I couldn't stand the pain anymore. I shut myself in a room, lay on the floor and shouted to the Lord, "I am not leaving here until You do something. Kill me, heal me, but don't let me suffer like this!" It was a little later, and then I heard a still, small voice saying, "Peace I leave with you; my peace I give you. I do not give to you as the world gives. Do not let your hearts be troubled and do not be afraid" (John 14:27).*

Michael was encouraged by John 14:27 because when God gives peace, He is imparting a sense of the Prince of Peace, His Son Jesus. Michael tells me he can endure almost anything, as long as he knows Jesus is "lying on the floor" with him. And as Psalm 119:49 assures, God's comfort envelops Michael every time he remembers a promise like that from the Word:

> Remember your word to your servant,
>   for you have given me hope.
> My comfort in my suffering is this:
>   Your promise preserves my life.

That doesn't mean that God lets you out of your cramped corner in life, that the pain goes away, the paralysis is healed, or the depression suddenly evaporates. But it does mean that in the tightest, most confining of life circumstances, you and I can find a wide place to stand in the sweet presence and sustaining might of a God who loves us beyond measure.

I can identify. For me, when the pain doesn't go away, I'm quick to remember promises like John 14:27. My comfort in my suffering is this: the promise of God's presence preserves my life. The walls may be God's walls, but the hope I experience is God's hope!

Despair that rises in a direct and vertical line to God opens us up to change, real hope, and the possibility of seeing God as He really is, not as we want Him to be. Once we give an inch, God will take a mile. He'll take a million miles. He'll soar on the wings of the wind from heaven to where you are to show you who He is, to embrace you with His love.

Just knowing He's with me gives me peace, hope, and comfort.

Here is the ruby, hard-won. Just knowing He's with me gives me peace, hope, and comfort. I may be confined, but I am not cramped. I have freedom to move when there is no freedom to move. I have breathing room when I'm about to suffocate. I stand in a wide, spacious place when I'm impaled by a thorny, encircling hedge of pain.

Resurrection

The circumstances Paul described in the province of Asia—whatever they may have been—took him right to the edge. Different translators of Scripture reached for the right combination of English words to describe what he had experienced.

> We were completely overwhelmed; the burden was more than we could bear. (PHILLIPS)

> We were so utterly and unbearably weighed down and crushed that we despaired even of life. (AMPLIFIED)

> It was so bad we didn't think we were going to make it. (THE MESSAGE)

> We were excessively pressed beyond our power, so as to despair even of living. (DARBY)

Why did God allow the apostle and his company to be pressured and pressed to the point of suffocation? We don't have to wonder. Paul immediately provides us with the answer.

> But this happened that we might not rely on ourselves but on God, who raises the dead. He has delivered us from such a deadly peril, and he will deliver us. On him we have set our hope that he will continue to deliver us, as you help us by your prayers. (2 Corinthians 1:9–10)

That we might rely on Him.

Period.

In the heavy darkness of one of the blackest nights, at the very moment when the strain pushed Paul over the ragged edge of despair, something broke loose. Like summer thunder. Like a sudden rush of wind across a spring meadow. Like a towering tsunami of light.

Resurrection power.

Life in a graveyard.

A sunrise at midnight.

Hope where no hope could be.

A cluster of California poppies on the dark side of the moon.

A surge of strength in utter weakness.

The resurrection power of the indwelling Christ.

We think of Jesus, the eternal, omnipresent, all powerful Son of God who willingly stepped into the constraints of time and space, the constraints of a tiny Roman province called Palestine, and the constraints of a human body. Eventually, betrayed into the power of His enemies, they constrained Him to a cross—literally nailed Him into place while adversaries mocked and demons danced. And then the very Author of life gave himself over to the ultimate constraints of death, tightly wound burial cloths, and a sealed tomb.

But it couldn't hold Him.

He broke free of death, pushed aside the stone, and demonstrated once and for all to everyone who has ever been boxed in by circumstances that there is life—room to breathe, room to run—in union with Him.

Never Alone

And there they go.

What I just did was the hardest thing ... staying casual and cheerful while they tied on bandanas, laced up hiking boots, and filled canteens. I know they felt bad for me, staying alone here in camp. (They kept glancing at me out of the corners of their eyes, to see if I was really okay with it.) But I also know that this is Jasper National Park in the Canadian Rockies, and who knows if we'll ever be back. I could tell they were itching to get some hard exercise, to get their hearts pumping and explore the ridge together. I can hear their voices a quarter mile away—sound carries at this high elevation in the clear mountain air. Kathy and Jay, my sisters, off together to conquer the ridge line on the shoulder of Whistler's Mountain—and then to walk up the mountain as far as they can go. They'll be gone for hours.

How I ache to go with them.

I thought I just heard Kathy's laugh as they climb the trail. There they are ... two colored dots moving up the ridge. Kathy's gold vest, and Jay's red. And now they're over the ridge and out of sight.

I have been trying so hard not to ruin this camping trip for everyone by getting depressed or feeling sorry for myself. Dad and Mom are off in the village, getting supplies, maybe a cup of coffee, looking around, just enjoying being together. And my sisters are talking and laughing up beyond me somewhere, seeing the world from a higher place.

I told them I'd be fine, that I really wanted to read, and would enjoy the peace and quiet. They propped up a book for me, but after they'd gone, my first attempt to turn the dog-eared page with a shrug of my shoulder and arm splint sent the book facedown into the dirt. It's still there. I can't get at it or do anything about it. Now I'll just have to wait until somebody gets back.

But I want to explore too. I was always the daredevil, pushing life to the edge, doing crazy stunts on horseback, challenging myself to do more. And now I just want to feel the trail under my feet and the morning sun on my face, warming my hair and the tops of my shoulders. I want to smell the fir trees, and the dust kicked up on the trail. I want to breathe hard, feel my leg muscles burn from the climb and the sweat pop out on my back. I want to look west from a high vista and see the peaks of these Northern Rockies on the horizon.

Mostly, I just want to be with Kath and Jay. And laugh. And talk about normal things. Silly things.

I can't help it. I just feel so alone.

God help me, please. For their sake . . . don't let me fall back again.

Sometimes I can feel myself getting too close to the edge of that cliff, and I don't want to go there. I've been there too many times over the last two years, and it's a long, long fall. Every time it's happened, I've wondered if I would ever climb out again.

Day after day, I would just stay in bed and ask Mom to leave the lights out and the door closed. Listening to the steady hum of the air conditioner, I daydreamed of the days on my feet, how things felt in my hands and fingers, and all the things I used to do and can never, never do again in this world. The awful finality of it all! And then I would feel the room tilting and I would be sliding downward toward that pit, where there's no light, no air, that evil place where all those demons lurk, the ones that tormented me in the hospital. If I ever hit bottom, I don't know what would happen. Maybe I'd go crazy. Maybe I'd never come back to sanity.

So I can't do that. Can't go there. I *can't*. But it's so quiet and everyone's been gone so long, and they're all having fun, and I'm lonely. I guess it's funny. I can't feel anything below my neck, but I can sure feel this ache in my heart, like a spear going right through me. Sometimes I wish that part of me was paralyzed too.

FORTY YEARS LATER

In my office, at Joni and Friends.

I knew better. I knew I wasn't alone. Even then. I knew God was with me. Young as I was, I already had a history of witnessing God's kindness and faithfulness in my life. And today, some four decades later, I'm as sure of His presence as I'm sure of the sky above and the earth below. I *know* the truth. I *know* the promises. And I can quote you chapter and verse.

> God has said,
>> "Never will I leave you;
>> never will I forsake you."
> So we say with confidence,
>> "The Lord is my helper; I will not be afraid.
>> What can man do to me?"
>
> (Hebrews 13:5)

Then Jesus came to them and said, . . . "Surely I am with you always, to the very end of the age." (Matthew 28:18, 20)

> So do not fear, for I am with you;
>> do not be dismayed, for I am your God.
> I will strengthen you and help you;
>> I will uphold you with my righteous right hand.
>
> (Isaiah 41:10)

Words like these aren't just sweet sentiments or pretty poetry, like something you'd see surrounded by glitter on a Christian greeting card. They are true. I know — and know that I know — because I have stood on them for years. I've clung to them in countless storms, like a strong rope when I felt myself slipping. God's words to me have been refined in my heart through years of testing and trials, growing ever more precious.

> *The words of the LORD are flawless,*
> *like silver refined in a furnace of clay,*
> *purified seven times.*
>
> (Psalm 12:6)

Even so, in times of grief or loss, in the grip of great fear or physical pain, we can know all the promises of His presence and His care, and yet still feel the darkness, still feel alone.

Darkness in My Path ...

A sixteenth-century friar known to history as Saint John of the Cross called it "the dark night of the soul." He should know. Because of his efforts at reformation within the Carmelite order to which he belonged, he was publicly humiliated and flogged by his superiors, and then imprisoned for days on end in a cell barely larger than his body.

Looking back on some of these truly awful experiences, he wrote: "Spiritual persons suffer great trials from the fear of being lost on the road and that God has abandoned them...."

Lost on the road.

Abandoned by God.

Maybe you've had one of those "dark night" experiences. Not long ago I found myself right in the middle of one. I had been in bed for over two months, suffering from searing, nonstop pain in my neck.

Friends were kind enough during that long ordeal, and my husband Ken was good enough to read the Bible by my bedside, but it was like listening through earplugs. Everything sounded muffled and distant. It was a time, as Job put it, "where even the light is like darkness" (10:22).

Eventually, visiting friends would take their leave, and my husband would close the Bible, kiss me, and say goodnight. With the lights out and the pain like a smoldering fire, I would lie there in the quiet, a darkness settling over me that was blacker than the mere absence of light.

In Job 19:8, it says, "He has blocked my way so I cannot pass; he has shrouded my path in darkness." And then Jeremiah mourned in the book of Lamentations, "He has made me dwell in darkness" (3:6).

I'm not Job, I'm not Jeremiah, and I'm not John of the Cross … but I can empathize.

I have learned through the years that experiences like these are just part of the process of growing in the Lord Jesus. Difficulty, struggle, and feelings of loneliness are bound to be part of the hedge with which God has enclosed those who suffer—so we must learn not to be dismayed in the face of darkness.

When light seems to be denied us we find ourselves crying out with the writer of Psalm 77. Who knows what dark night of the soul had come upon Asaph, the author of this psalm. Was he being persecuted? Was he fighting a lingering illness that wracked his body with pain? Was he grieving over a wayward child or maybe the death of his wife of many years? Was he sick with worry over the future? Was he wrestling with demonic oppression? The Bible doesn't tell us. But most of us, at one time or another in our lives, could have written the words he penned in the deep crisis of heart.

> *I cried out to God for help;*
> *I cried out to God to hear me.*

> *When I was in distress, I sought the Lord;*
>   *at night I stretched out untiring hands*
>   *and my soul refused to be comforted.*
>
> *I remembered you, O God, and I groaned;*
>   *I mused, and my spirit grew faint.*
> *You kept my eyes from closing;*
>   *I was too troubled to speak. . . .*
>
> *Will the Lord reject forever?*
>   *Will he never show his favor again?*
> *Has his unfailing love vanished forever?*
>   *Has his promise failed for all time?*
> *Has God forgotten to be merciful?*
>   (Psalm 77:1–4, 7–9)

When we find ourselves crying out, "Has God forgotten to be gracious? Has He forgotten His love for me?" the Bible has a remedy, a prescription, a medicine for melancholy—we are to remember and remember and remember again the way God worked in the past.

In the same psalm, perhaps brushing away his tears, Asaph put it this way:

> *I call to remembrance my song in the night;*
>   *I meditate within my heart. . .*
>
> *I will remember the works of the LORD;*
>   *Surely I will remember Your wonders of old.*
> *I will also meditate on all Your work,*
>   *And talk of Your deeds.*
>   (Psalm 77:6, 11–12 NKJV)

You see, the psalmist realized that his darkness lay in his own infirmity, not in his God. The loneliness and sense of isolation would come over him like a cloud covering the moon on a starless night. And when it did, he would remember, he would meditate, and he would talk out loud of all God had done for him.

So that's what I do.

That has been my practice when my pain and the darkness try to push me into a lonely corner. I talk of His deeds. Right out loud.

That's what I did on those sleepless nights of neck pain. Mouthing the words quietly, so as not to awaken Ken, I whispered all the wonderful ways God had revealed Himself to me in days gone by.

God, You were with me at that youth camp so long ago, under the Virginia stars. I sat on that big flat rock and reached out to You and You were there.

Jesus, You were with me when I was facedown in that Stryker frame, fighting off those demons. You spoke to me through the pages of Your word right there on the hospital floor, as I turned the pages with a stick in my mouth.

You were with me in my loneliness and the ache of my loss on that camping trip, when my sisters scaled the mountain in the morning sunshine, leaving me alone in camp.

You were with me on that cold winter night in Wichita, when I was pitched face first out of my wheelchair onto the icy asphalt of the parking lot. It was You who enabled me to keep going when I wanted to quit, to fulfill my speaking engagement the very next night, and to declare Your love and faithfulness.

Praise You, Lord, You were with me when Ken Tada walked into my life, dark, handsome, and strong, with a twinkle in his eye and a smile that lit up a room.

You were with me at the orphanage on that dark afternoon in Bucharest, when I held the dying child in my arms and wheeled around and around that dreary room as the rain beat against the windows. I sang to him, that weak, frail little boy, and my heart was breaking. You sang, too, because he didn't die after all. He was adopted by a family in California and has become a strong, healthy young man who knows You and loves You.

I remembered, and the memories came like a flood. The songs in the night ... the tender mercies ... the miracles ... the still, small

voice of the Holy Spirit ... the giant baby steps of triumph my severely disabled friends have taken, doing their best, showing courage, leaning on Jesus ... the sweet moments in beautiful places all
over the world with family and loved ones ... and Ken, my other
half, my soul mate, my best friend.

I remembered how Jesus took up our infirmities and carried our
diseases, how He understands and sympathizes with my weakness.
And how He considers my frail frame and remembers that, after all,
I'm only dust. I remembered, remembered, and remembered again.

Do Not Forget ...

This discipline of remembering is so important to the Lord—and
to us.

In the book of Exodus, the Israelites broke out into a spontaneous praise song to the Lord after He opened a path through the Red
Sea. You can imagine their amazement when they saw the water
parted like giant glass skyscrapers. Little wonder they sang on for
twenty-one verses in music and melody.

> *I will sing to the LORD,*
>   *for he is highly exalted. . . .*
> *The LORD is my strength and my song;*
>   *he has become my salvation.*
> *He is my God, and I will praise him. . . .*
>   (Exodus 15:1, 2)

But just a few verses later, their joy turned sour.

Their song gave out after three days traveling in the desert without finding water. They grumbled, saying, "What are we to drink?"
The songs faded all too quickly when they ran into trouble. The
irony is, they grumbled about *water.* Didn't they remember God's
miracle with water? They'd just seen a whole sea of it!

And so it is with us. Our own songs of praise fade all too quickly when we forget how God protects and provides for us. We need to take the advice God gave the Israelites in Deuteronomy 4:9: "Only be careful, and watch yourselves closely so that you do not forget the things your eyes have seen."

I challenge you to put this to the test. When you find yourself slipping into anxiety or depression, begin speaking aloud your praise and gratitude to God for specific instances of His grace in your life. Or if you are so inclined, make it a spontaneous song, like the Israelites sang on the other side of the Red Sea.

This isn't the old, trite cliché of "count your blessings name them one by one." This is an authentic, viable spiritual transaction between you and the God who listens and considers your every word.

Go back to that time when you were overwhelmed by your sin and shame and sought His forgiveness and restoration. Tell Him (out loud) how He freed you from your guilt and brought a sweet peace into your innermost being.

Tell Him (verbally) about the time when you were in danger and could easily have been injured or killed if God hadn't stepped in to rescue you.

Recall with Him (in spoken words) that season of confusion and perplexity in your life, when you didn't know whether to go forward, backward, or sideways. Tell Him you remember how He placed a firm but gentle hand on your shoulder, whispering in your ear, "This is the way, walk in it" (Isaiah 30:21).

Speak to Him about those days when you were so lonely that it felt like a physical pain gripping your heart. Remember with Him how His Spirit came alongside, whispering hope — or prompted one of your friends "out of the blue" to make a surprise phone call because they were "just thinking about you."

Call these things to mind. You know very well they weren't happenstance or coincidence. That was *God* at work in your life. Voice your gratitude aloud. It's very, very powerful. In fact, remembering has been God's remedy for His people through thousands of years.

Remember how the LORD your God led you all the way in the desert.... (Deuteronomy 8:2)

Remember that you were slaves ... and the LORD your God redeemed you.... (Deuteronomy 24:18)

Remember the Lord, who is great and awesome, and fight for your brothers, your sons and your daughters, your wives and your homes. (Nehemiah 4:14)

> *On my bed I remember you;*
> *I think of you through the watches of the night.*
> *Because you are my help,*
> *I sing in the shadow of your wings.*
>
> (Psalm 63:6–7)

> *I remember your ancient laws, O LORD,*
> *and I find comfort in them.*
>
> (Psalm 119:52)

> *Remember the LORD in a distant land,*
> *and think on Jerusalem.*
>
> (Jeremiah 51:50)

"Don't you remember? When I broke the five loaves for the five thousand, how many basketfuls of pieces did you pick up?" (Mark 8:18–19)

Remember Jesus Christ, raised from the dead, descended from David. This is my gospel, for which I am suffering. (2 Timothy 2:8–9)

Remember those earlier days after you had received the light, when you stood your ground in a great contest in the face of suffering. (Hebrews 10:32)

Remember the height from which you have fallen! Repent and do the things you did at first. (Revelation 2:5)

Here is the ruby, hard-won. When nothing seems to be happening in the moment, when loneliness settles over your spirit like a lead apron, when pain and grief and anxiety conspire to push you to the edge of despair, remember God's mighty deeds in your life. Remember His kindness, His special, tailor-made graces that fell out of the sky like a gentle spring rain.

> *Remember His kindness, His special, tailor-made graces that fell out of the sky like a gentle spring rain.*

A Presence in the Night

Sometimes in those mad, midnight moments when hope recedes, worries mount, and sleep refuses to come, I have to remind myself that God isn't sleeping, either. He hasn't caught a wink. He sits up with me all night. He hears me when no one else hears me, bending down to listen to my whisper. He knows every tear that falls from my eye, every thought that flits across my mind, every expression on my face in the darkness.

He is awake.

> *He who watches over you will not slumber;*
> *indeed, he who watches over Israel*
> *will neither slumber nor sleep.*
>
> (Psalm 121:3–4)

Sometimes at night when I hear Ken stir in the bed, I will whisper, "Are you awake?" Maybe when we find ourselves wakeful in the wee hours of the morning, we should whisper that same question to God. *"Are You awake? Do You want to talk?"* The answer is yes and yes. He is certainly awake and alert, never groggy or drowsy, never disturbed by my call in the night, and always ready to talk to me and be a companion to me.

Three things happen to me all night long.

Three things happen to me when I feel the ache of loneliness.

The Father is awake and watches over me. He watches over my going out and coming in. He is behind me and before me and lays His hand over me.

The Spirit is awake and helps me in my weakness, praying prayers for me beyond what I could begin to conceive, and with groans that words cannot express. His very name, Counselor, means someone who comes alongside to help.

And Jesus ... He is awake too. He is ever my Advocate, the Counsel for my defense, the One who faces down every lying tongue in hell, the One who speaks to the Father on my behalf, and who also prays for me.

Have you ever had anyone put a hand on your shoulder and pray for you — sincerely and earnestly intercede for you — perhaps with a broken voice and through tears? At different times in my travels around the world I have brought a prayer team with me — women who have a proven ministry in intercession. Time and time again these prayer warriors have placed their hands on me and prayed for me before critical meetings and in times of physical weakness and before speaking opportunities and television appearances. What a comfort that is, and what a bond that builds between people!

But even though my prayer team is only with me on certain occasions, the Bible says that both the Holy Spirit and Jesus, God's Son, pray for me constantly, even in those moments when I am so deep in the darkness or crushed by loneliness that I can't pray for myself.

Not all aloneness, of course, is loneliness.

We need to remember that too.

Strange as it may seem, there have been some days lately when I wanted to be away from everyone else, by myself, and alone with God. There are days when I'd like to rewrite the words of the old hymn "I Need Thee Every Hour." With me, it's more like every *minute*. Oh, the comfort of feeling desperate for Jesus!

I'm sure you've had days like that, in which you feel as though you must cling to Him every minute, every sixty seconds. That's when I carve out time to be alone with Him. I don't take phone-calls, I cancel my luncheon date, I turn off my cell phone, and I close the office door just to be with God.

You can transact life-shaping business with God when you're alone with Him. Look at the record:

Jacob was alone when he crossed the Jabbok and spent the night wrestling with the Angel of the Lord.

Moses was alone when the Lord revealed Himself through the burning bush, giving an old man a fresh vision for life and a great work to accomplish.

Joshua was alone when he met a warrior angel prior to the attack on Jericho.

Manoah's wife was alone in the field when the angel of the Lord appeared to her and gave her news about the baby she was to bear—a boy named Samson.

Isaiah was alone when he received his commission from the Lord, saw the Lord high and lifted up, and tasted the burning coals of holiness on his tongue.

Elisha was alone when the mantle of the prophet fell across his shoulders.

Paul was alone in the Arabian desert when the Lord gave him personal instructions about preaching the Word.

Mary was alone when the angel brought her the message that she would give birth to the Savior.

John was alone—exiled—on the island of Patmos when he received his matchless revelation of things to come.

If you need a word from the Lord—direction, help, hope—set aside time to be alone with Him. Expect Him to speak to you. Guidance and real fellowship only come in those times of solitude, in an hour when you say to the Lord, "I need You."

We Must Do the Work ...

Sometimes we can feel lonely in our responsibilities and duties. Ever feel like you're the only one holding it all together? Nobody seems to be worried about the things that worry you. If you didn't make that call or write that note, who would?

Did it ever occur to you that you have somebody on your side who's taking more than His fair share of the load? In the ninth chapter of the gospel of John, Jesus was conversing with His disciples —and with a man who had been blind from birth. The disciples opened the dialogue with a question:

> "Rabbi, who sinned, this man or his parents, that he was born blind?"
>
> "Neither this man nor his parents sinned," said Jesus, "but this happened so that the work of God might be displayed in his life." (John 9:2–3)

And then Jesus said a very curious thing.

> "As long as it is day, we must do the work of him who sent me. Night is coming, when no one can work." (John 9:4)

Who was Jesus talking to? I can't be sure ... but I have a strong feeling He was looking directly at that disabled man. "We ... *we* must do the work of Him who sent Me."

I choose to think that in that moment, Jesus was reminding the blind man that he was not alone. He was not alone in his disability, and he was not alone in his despair. In fact, the mighty works of God were about to be displayed through him and through his life. The Lord wanted this man to know that God Himself was standing by his side, taking on more than His fair share of the load.

Jesus went on to actually heal the man, of course, but I think the Lord's words alone must have thrilled him beyond telling. Jesus was siding with him, choosing him, saying, "We, my friend, must do the works of God. Together."

It awes me to think that Jesus wants to help me to help Him accomplish God's desires for this world. I'm not alone in it. I'm not leading a one-woman parade. I don't have to weaken under the pressure. It doesn't all fall on my sagging shoulders.

Christ stands with me — just as He stood with the blind man that day. And He's standing with you today too. Especially if you feel as though you're desperately holding together all the loose ends. Be comforted; it won't all fall apart without you. Jesus is saying to you, "We — *we* must do the works of God."

How can I be lonely in my work when Jesus has rolled up His sleeves to help me and partner with me?

If isolation and loneliness is not your lot in this season of life, ask God to reveal someone in your neighborhood or church to whom you can show His love, compassion, support, and friendship. Find a person who is wounded and hurting, and be to that man, be to that woman, be to that child the hands, heart, and smile of Christ Himself.

It may be a time in their lives they will treasure into eternity.

Sufficient Grace

I'm back in the van with the team from Prison Fellowship, looking out at the gray November landscape rushing by. I don't think anyone feels much like talking. A visit to the infamous DC Department of Corrections facility would be enough to make anyone feel a little down.

It didn't look like a jail as much as a grim, decaying army post. Row after row of low, flat, red-brick dormitories. Clutches of men, most in sweatpants and sneakers, walking the grounds, heading for meals and prison jobs.

What a ghastly place to wile away years and years of your life: in a crowded cage, behind barbed wire.

But there are brothers in the Lord in that cage, and I just spoke to eighty of them—in a cement-floored meeting room under the flicker of failing fluorescent lights. All of these guys have come to Christ since coming to prison, and they asked me to bring a word of encouragement to them.

As I looked into their eyes, I simply told my story and spoke about the sustaining grace of the Lord Jesus—how His power shows up best in our weakness. The men listened because they knew it was more than words with me, more than a nice speech or a canned sermon-for-the-prisoners. They could see my useless arms and legs. They could see my chair. They knew I'd been in this condition for eleven long years. They could appreciate the fact that I was a young woman whose life had drastically changed, with no going back. Without my even saying it, they made the association between their condition and mine. The difference was, some of them would be released from their prison, and I never will ... until I die.

As I spoke, most of the men nodded and said their amens.

Apparently I broke all kinds of protocol—and made the guards very nervous—when I asked a couple of the men to come up on the platform with me and sing "Amazing Grace."

Grace ... how desperately we need it.

Afterward, a group of them gathered around me, under the watchful eyes of stone-faced guards armed with lethal weapons. I asked several of them how much time they had yet to serve. Some had only a few months, others many years. I identified more with the guys who had another twenty or thirty years of confinement stretching out before them, with no hope of release.

Then, to that smaller group. I confessed something personal. Now I'm wondering if I should have said what I said.

I told them how weak-kneed I sometimes got when I thought about living twenty or even thirty more years in a wheelchair. A number of them nodded silently. I told them I had my own bolts and bars to live with—and how frightening it was to think of another *twenty years* this way.

So I identified with them—those guys thinking about decades behind bars and barbed wire in that run-down, overcrowded place. Even though they've come to terms with their circumstances, it's tough, sometimes even overwhelming, to face a future of confinement and limitations.

But I probably shouldn't have said all that.

I was supposed to be bringing a word of encouragement.

THIRTY YEARS LATER,
MY OFFICE IN AGOURA HILLS

I'll admit it, the long years haven't made paralysis any easier.

My disabilities have never become routine. Quadriplegia isn't something you "get used to" any more than blindness or severe chronic pain. You learn how to work with it and how to accomplish things in spite of it, but you can never wholly forget about it.

To this day I can only handle so much, and some days I feel like I'm right at my limit. Living in a wheelchair has a tendency to make even ordinary days seem overwhelming at times. My weak shoulder muscles ache from holding up my heavy head. My back gets tired from sitting in one position. My neck gets a crick in it from looking up at everybody standing around me. In 1978, there at Lorton Prison with Chuck Colson and his team, I wondered how I could ever manage twenty or thirty years like this.

And now it has been over forty.

How have I come this far? Has it been by my fortitude, my perseverance, or by my determination? No, it has been a work of God's grace from beginning to end.

Even so, who can help trying to glance down the road sometimes, wondering what's around the bend? Sometimes I look up on my wall calendar and gaze at the blank months of years to come and I wonder, *What will it be like five years from now? Ten years? Will I still be on this side of heaven? What if my husband suffers an injury and can't take care of me? Worse yet, I won't be able to take care of him!*

When I think about my deteriorating physical condition and the more and more frequent bouts of intolerable pain, I can feel the vertigo as strongly as the twenty-eight-year-old woman who spoke to those prisoners back in Maryland years ago.

What did I know of God's grace then? Maybe only a little, but it gave me what I needed to press on. I realized even then that God didn't expect me to accept what might or might not happen to me in twenty years.

"... And as thy days, so shall thy strength be" (Deuteronomy 33:25 KJV).

God doesn't give me grace for the future, uncertain seasons that He may grant me on earth before He takes me home. He doesn't give me grace for next year's headaches — or even next month's heartaches. He won't even loan me enough grace to face the prospects of tomorrow! God only gives me grace for today. He expects me to live *this* day in His strength, leaning on His wisdom, drawing on His presence and power.

As I write these words, I have a mental picture of my dad. I can see his eyes looking into mine. I can hear his voice saying to me, "Don't grasp for the future, Joni. Pay attention to the present." That's the way Daddy lived; that's the way he worked.

Whenever my dad would build stone walls on the farm, he wouldn't rush. He would pick up a rock, brush off the dirt, turn it over in his hands, and line it up this way and that, trying to place it just right. He paid attention to what he was doing at the moment. His whole focus was on fitting each stone. As a result, forty years later, the walls haven't crumbled. Daddy's labors have endured.

My stone-laying father would say it's the only way to live. We make the mistake of thinking God is always preparing us for "future ministry." We rush through the present moment too quickly in our effort to reach the next one. As a result, we don't pay sufficient attention to the immediate. Oswald Chambers has said, "Grace is for 'right now.' It is not the process toward some future goal, but an end in and of itself. If we would only realize this, then each moment would become rich with meaning and purpose."

In the book of Ephesians, as Paul was wrapping up a matchless document on the eternal purposes of God and His high goals for redeemed men and women, he wrote: "Be very careful, then, how you live—not as unwise but as wise, making the most of *every* opportunity, because the days are evil" (Ephesians 5:15, emphasis mine).

Other translations say, "Walk circumspectly," "Redeem the time," or "Make the most of each moment." God is interested in the situation we find ourselves in this instant. It's incidental that He may use our circumstances to prepare us for the future.

There is no more important moment in your life than this one.

It's easy to look at the month of November and start grasping for December. And before you know it, your thoughts are occupied with January and setting goals for the New Year. But that's no way to build a season, just as it's no way to build a wall.

Here is a ruby, hard-won through long years: We can't help glancing behind us at times to consider where we've been, and it's natural for us to wonder what awaits us around the bend. In fact, it's a wise and even biblical activity to plan ahead. But remember this: There is no more important moment in your life than this one.

Take it slowly. Look at today and, as my father would say, pay attention to what you do with it.

Who said it more clearly than Jesus Himself? "Therefore do not worry about tomorrow, for tomorrow will worry about itself. Each day has enough trouble of its own" (Matthew 6:34).

Living in "the Now"

If we fail to grasp this most basic perspective, no wonder we feel overwhelmed by life! When Jesus speaks of Satan, the enemy of our souls, he names him as one who "comes only to steal and kill and destroy" (John 10:10). When you think about it, if our adversary can get us to focus on our past mistakes, wrong turns, and wasted opportunities, he has stolen the present moment from us. And if he can nudge us into worry and anxiety over tomorrow's bills, tomorrow's deadlines, tomorrow's health concerns, he has done it again!

If our enemy can keep us occupied with our past or with our future, we lose the grace, blessings, and opportunities in the Now. And when you lose the present moment, in a sense you lose everything.

Why? Because now is all we have.

Life on earth is simply a string of consecutive moments, beginning on the day of our birth and terminating at the moment when God takes us home. Think of those moments—those precious moments of life—as pearls on a string, each loaded with potential and opportunity. The thief wants to rob you of as many of those pearls as possible. And he does that by causing you to live life in the rearview mirror, or concerning yourself with future scenarios that most likely will never occur.

Just recently, I heard an older man say, "I've had many crises in my life through many years—and most of them never happened."

When will we poor time-bound creatures learn? Life is lived in the moment. Praise ascends to God's throne in a moment. Self-pity, lust, and idolatry are defeated in a moment. Courage seizes an opportunity in a moment. Love reaches out in a moment. Faith takes its stand on the moment. Wisdom draws an insight from the Scriptures in a moment. Ideas that can impact the world flash by in a moment.

And we appropriate the grace of our God—in full and generous supply—moment by moment by moment. One day at a time. Redeeming each hour. Drawing on His grace like a tulip opening to April sunlight, like oxygen in the bloodstream, like life itself. And leaving the future to Him.

I know a man named Chris whose life drives this point home to me. Chris is a middle-aged man with Down syndrome who lives with his folks. He enjoys volunteering with Awana and taking part in various socials at church. And he's blessed with an unusual gift. He has no concept of time. Every day for Chris is the same as the day before.

I know it's frustrating for Chris at times, but I call it a gift because every day is the day of salvation for Chris. A faithful church-goer, Chris listens intently to the messages, whether they be light and whimsical or heavy with fire and brimstone. And on days when a speaker gives a stirring invitation to join the family of God, Chris is usually heard to remark to a nearby elder after the service, "I accepted Him today! I accepted Him!" His face shines and his eyes overflow with tears.

Skeptics and cynics would tell you that Chris hasn't got a clue what he's doing. If he knew, they would argue, he'd realize how unnecessary it is to be saved more than once. Chris doesn't see it that way. And God doesn't either. Both the Lord and Chris are able to enjoy that blessed gift of now-ness. Every past moment of conviction of sin, for Chris, gets poured into the now. Every hope he has of heaven and having a new body and mind gets poured into the now. And the feeling is overwhelming for him.

Some days I wish I could shed myself of time and live as Chris does — enjoying God's sense of now-ness. I know I've been called to build upon and move past the foundation of salvation, but to recall those broken and tender moments of joy for the first time — *that* would be blessed.

I knew that much at least in 1978, and God has been faithful. But there was — and is — so much more to learn about grace ... and how it intersects with our weakness and need.

Leaning on Grace

A friend of mine lives near the Columbia River, one of the mighty watercourses of the world, flowing at 122.7 million gallons per minute. (How in the world do they measure such things?) One day this past summer while he was walking along a river trail, he happened to notice a tiny sparrow alight on the very edge of that great river and dip its little beak in the water. Just once. Satisfied, it flew away.

He told me it made him think of God's grace. He felt as if the

Lord was saying to him, "You are like that little bird, taking a tiny sip of a river more vast than you will ever understand. My grace is that much greater than your need."

I know that's true. But then again, it is our need that *drives* us to the river!

J. I. Packer wrote:

> God uses chronic pain and weakness, along with other afflictions, as his chisel for sculpting our lives. Felt weakness deepens dependence on Christ for strength each day. The weaker we feel, the harder we lean. And the harder we lean, the stronger we grow spiritually, even while our bodies waste away. To live with your "thorn" uncomplainingly — that is, sweet, patient, and free in heart to love and help others, even though every day you feel weak — is *true* sanctification. It is true healing for the spirit. It is a supreme victory of grace.[1]

The weaker we feel, the harder we lean. And the harder we lean, the stronger we grow.

Extraordinary stamina, you say? A testimony to human courage, maybe? Remarkable grit and perseverance?

Not even close. Grit-your-teeth stamina and human courage have nothing to do with experiencing His grace. It isn't human strength that prompts God to pour out His grace, it is human *weakness*. Complete dependence.

Dr. Packer goes on to explain that the main aim of God in the work of grace is "an ever deeper knowledge of God, and ever closer fellowship with Him. Grace is God drawing us sinners closer and closer to himself."[2]

In the long run, how does He do that? By shielding us? By deflecting every assault from the world, the flesh, and the devil? By protecting us from difficult, even heartbreaking circumstances? Will growing grace in our lives look like sunnier days, increasing success, and a smoother ride?

No, in fact He may accomplish it in our lives by exposing us to difficulty and trouble, allowing us to be overwhelmed with a sense of our own inadequacy. As a result, we cling to the Lord more closely, more tenaciously—for simple survival!

As one paraphrase renders Paul's words to the Corinthians:

> I quit focusing on the handicap and began appreciating the gift. It was a case of Christ's strength moving in on my weakness. Now I take limitations in stride, and with good cheer, these limitations that cut me down to size—abuse, accidents, opposition, bad breaks. I just let Christ take over! And so the weaker I get, the stronger I become. (2 Corinthians 12:9–10, THE MESSAGE)

This is the ultimate reason, from our standpoint, why God permits heartaches and perplexities of one sort and another into our lives: it is to ensure that we learn to *hold Him fast.*

Dr. Packer says:

> When we walk along a clear road feeling fine, and someone takes our arm to help us, as likely as not we shall impatiently shake him off; but when we are caught on a rough country road in the dark, with a storm getting up and our strength spent, and someone takes our arm to help us, we shall lean thankfully on him.[3]

You might have a tough time living with your weakness today. You find it nearly impossible to be "sweet and patient and free in heart to love and help others."

Please hear me on this, a woman who has lived with total paralysis for 14,965 days (give or take). It isn't difficult, it isn't daunting, it isn't a great challenge, it isn't nearly impossible.

It *is* impossible.

You simply can't manage sweet patience and true joy while you're trying to find within yourself the stamina or courage to do so. You will fail every time. The courage, the patience, and the will to get up and face each day come from another Source, outside yourself and yet within you. Felt weakness should deepen our dependence upon the grace and strength of Christ. Remember, the weaker you feel, the harder you must lean on Jesus. And leaning means trusting, obeying, spending concentrated time talking to Him, and sharing your deepest needs.

When you lean that hard, you'll find yourself growing stronger than you ever dreamed possible. And you will also begin to see how grace relates to that increasingly rare and elusive state of being we call contentment.

The Secret of Contentment

I am not saying this because I am in need, for I have learned to be content whatever the circumstances. I know what it is to be in need, and I know what it is to have plenty. I have learned the secret of being content in any and every situation, whether well fed or hungry, whether living in plenty or in want. (Philippians 4:11–12)

I saw a man in the supermarket yesterday using a new sporty wheelchair. When he zipped down the aisle, his chair didn't make a squeak. I glanced down at my big, clunky, decades-old model with dirt on the frame and threadbare padding. Little wonder I looked with envy at his high-tech wheels.

I'd like a trade-in on my wheelchair. Perhaps you would like a trade-in on your old car. Or maybe the grass seems greener down the street where they are building brand new homes. Yes, an automatic garage door opener and a trash compactor would be great to have. But sometimes when we compile our desires up against God's desires for us, I wonder how many match.

The apostle Paul described contentment as a secret. Something hidden from view, concealed from knowledge.

What secret was he talking about?

That's one of those questions people like to throw out at small groups or Bible studies to stimulate a little discussion. But it's more than a mildly engaging topic to talk about over bad coffee and day-old doughnuts.

If you happen to find yourself in a maximum security prison facing a third of your life behind bars ... if you wake up to the cold, unyielding fact of marriage to a spouse who truly only cares about himself ... if you discover that your long-awaited, much-prayed-for baby has Down syndrome ... if that stable company cuts you loose in your mid-fifties from your once-secure position, leaving you with few prospects ... if any of those things are true, or any of ten thousand other heartaches, then "what's the secret" is more than an intellectually stimulating question.

It is life itself.

And when you're without it — the secret of contentment — there isn't much left except despair, or "lives of quiet desperation," as Thoreau once put it. And sometimes the desperation isn't quiet at all. On a hot, humid night in July, eight years after I visited Lorton Prison, hundreds of inmates set fire to thirteen of those overcrowded dormitories, forcing the temporary evacuation of more than eight hundred prisoners to even more-crowded, higher-security cellblocks. Twenty-nine inmates, nine guards, and six firefighters were injured. One inmate later died.

What was Paul's secret of contentment? He gave it away in the next breath when he said that he was ready for anything through the strength of the One who lived inside him. Contentment is found not in circumstances. Contentment is found in a Person, the Lord Jesus. Just this morning I began a reading of the book of Philippians and only got as far as the second verse: "Grace and peace to you from God our Father and the Lord Jesus Christ."

Yes, it was perhaps a common greeting among Christians in that day. But it is also an elemental, rock-solid fact of life. Grace and peace have a source, and that source is not my situation or some pleasurable arrangement of my circumstances. If I am to have grace and peace — or true contentment — in my life at all, it will only be because it has flowed into my soul from the God and Father who loves me and the Savior and Friend who stands beside me.

How we need this abundant, free-flowing stream! It requires a special act of grace to accommodate ourselves to every condition of life, to carry an equal temper of mind through every circumstance. On the one hand, only in Christ can we face poverty contentedly, that is, without losing our comfort in God. On the other hand, only in Christ can we face plenty and not be filled with pride.

The New Testament word translated *contentment* in our English Bibles means "sufficiency." I've been told that Paul uses the same Greek root here in Philippians that he does in 2 Corinthians 12:9, where he says God's grace is sufficient.

What a secret, this working of grace in our lives! Beyond our normal comprehension. Hidden from our view. Hard to explain. Impossible to pinpoint. Difficult to understand.

Even so, you know it when you see it.

A friend of mine named Susan recently experienced unbearable pain with the sudden, unexpected breakup of her marriage. Even after a year, she's still picking up the pieces, the few fragments her husband left her when he broke their marriage vows for another woman. I watched Susan go through months of agony, struggling against rejection and just plain nausea.

But God's grace sustained her in a startling way. In fact, she commented to me just the other day that she believed the hardest thing to explain was how grace was at work in her life. To her, and to those of us who watched the tragedy unfold, the sustaining, preserving, uplifting power of God's grace was truly a mystery — a wondrous secret none of us could understand. All we could say was that God's grace was working. It was sufficient. For Susan, Jesus was enough.

Paul learned the secret of contentment. Susan is still learning the secret. Have hope. Take hold. He is sufficient.

Pressing into Grace

So what are we talking about here? Name-it-and-claim-it content-ment? Easy grace, turned on like a water tap whenever you feel like it? Is Christ some sort of magic wand you wave over your problems to make them disappear?

No. That's not what I see in Scripture.

The grace of God is abundant, boundless, inexhaustible, avail-able, and free. But it didn't come cheap.

It's not like a tepid puddle of water lying on the surface of soggy ground. It's a mighty underground river, rushing clear and fresh. And if you look for it, you'll find it. It's not like the feeble stir of air created by an electric fan in a warm room. It's a strong wind, wild and free, cresting mountaintops and blowing across a thousand fields and forests. But you have to step outside to feel it.

In Genesis 15, God speaks to Abram in a vision while he lay in his tent. But to see the full intent of the Lord's heart, Abram had to push back the covers, leave the comfort of his tent, walk out into the night — and see his descendants in the stars, like dust.

In Colossians 2:3, Paul speaks about "all the treasures of wisdom and knowledge" being hidden in Christ. Hidden? That calls to mind searching for buried treasure. In other words, it takes some effort. To search for something concealed requires work. In the book of Jeremiah, the Lord said: "You will seek me and find me when you seek me with all your heart" (Jeremiah 29:13).

Paul not only wrote "I can do everything through him who gives me strength" (Philippians 4:13), but he had to master it as well. It meant making tough choices — deciding this, not that; going in this direction, not that one. Why does it involve such hard work? Because it's not our natural bent. Seeking the hidden treasure of contentment in Christ doesn't come automatically. Just look at a few of Paul's well chosen words: "press on ... strive ... stand firm."

Here is a ruby, hard-won. As we wrap our hands around a

problem and in faith press on, strive, and stand firm, divine energy surges through us. We experience the fullness of His grace. We *press* into grace.

In other words, you make the hard choices; God gives you the grace.

He gives you the grace to hold your tongue when you feel you have cause for complaining—but you must choose to receive it. He imparts grace to look out for another's interest before your own—but you must deliberately step into that enabling. He infuses the grace to choose a bright attitude when you wake up in the morning—but your first smile of the day may have to be in faith.

As we wrap our hands around a problem and in faith press on, strive, and stand firm, divine energy surges through us.

What will your choices be? That answer will be as varied as there are people in the world. First Peter 4:10 describes the manifold—literally, many-colored—grace of God. The grace God brings to your life today is hand tailored and custom designed for your individual needs.

God's grace is not one-size-fits-all. He relates to you as an individual—a unique person created in His image. Don't fall into the trap of comparing your situation to that of others. Tell your Father your specific needs and desires, and He will fulfill you as no one else ever could.

You have the secret: as you press in, as you press on, He will give you grace.

Learning Grace

We seek the grace of God, we press into it, but we also *learn* it.

To learn something means more than mouthing the words "His grace is sufficient for me." *To learn* means to make choices, to practice over and over. If you are to know contentment—that quietness of heart growing out of supernatural grace that gladly submits to God in all circumstances—you must undergo the learning process.

I think back to the time years ago when I was newly injured and learning to feed myself for the first time. I can't tell you how many times I felt like giving up. Wearing a bib, smearing applesauce all over my clothes, and having it land more times on my lap than in my mouth was humiliating.

Who would have blamed me if I had thrown in the towel, claimed my injury was too profound, and said feeding myself would be out of the question? "Poor thing, she's really helpless. Isn't that sad?" And if I had made that decision then, would I have been feeding myself now? Would I even be alive?

God's grace was certainly there for me, but He wasn't going to force-feed me. It was up to me to make a series of tough choices. Was I going to let embarrassment over my food-smeared face dissuade me? Would I let disappointing failures overwhelm me? I'm convinced God gave me the strength to lift that spoon to my mouth. As a result, I did learn to feed myself, and today I manage a spoon quite well.

Did that mean I got back the use of my arms or hands?

No.

But drawing on His grace, I did learn to be content.

When Christ gives us strength to tackle a painful situation, gaining contentment doesn't mean losing sorrow or saying good-bye to discomfort. You can be sorrowful yet always rejoicing. You can have nothing and yet possess everything. First Timothy 6:6 says, "Godliness with contentment is great gain." Yet the gain always comes through loss. The grace always comes through need.

Don't let anyone tell you that contentment comes easily. It is not passive. In fact, it is gritty determination. It has to be *learned*. And it requires grace from beyond this world.

Grow in Grace

Peter wrote, "But grow in the grace and knowledge of our Lord and Savior Jesus Christ" (2 Peter 3:18).

How do you know if you've grown in grace through the years? How does anyone know that he or she is growing in grace? Is it something that can be measured? Bishop J. C. Ryle puts it this way:

> When I speak of growth in grace, I mean an increase in the degree, size, strength, vigor and power of the graces which the Spirit plants in our hearts. When I speak of a person growing in grace, I mean simply this — that his sense of sin is becoming deeper, his faith stronger, his hope brighter, his love more extensive and his spiritual-mindedness more marked. He feels more of the power of godliness in his heart. He manifests more of it in his life. He goes on from strength to strength, faith to faith, and from grace to grace.

I believe that means we can — and we should — see a change in our lives. Yes, I would say that my sense of sin is deeper than it was this time last year. My hope is brighter. And yes, I do seem to see things more through spiritual eyes. I would say that I truly do feel more of the power of godliness in my heart, and I pray that it shows up in my life in a way that others can see.

As we behold Him through prayer and study of His Word, we are transformed from strength to strength, from faith to faith, and from grace to grace. As it says in 2 Corinthians 3:18: "And we, who with unveiled faces all reflect the Lord's glory, are being transformed into his likeness with ever-increasing glory."

Another way to grow in God's grace is by simply allowing it to control my responses to a million everyday situations.

I think of a recent Saturday when a number of us gathered to help a new family who had moved into our church community. Friends from the congregation set aside a Saturday, donned their grubbies, and brought brushes, ladders, and paint to spiff up the place.

Ken and I arrived early, he with his white painting pants on and me with a bucket of paint in my lap. But as I wheeled through the front door, I realized my wheelchair presented an obstacle to people on ladders and stools.

I had a choice. Was I going to feel sorry for myself because I couldn't take part? Or was I going to listen to Hebrews 12:15? "See to it that no one misses the grace of God and that no bitter root grows up to cause trouble and defile many."

I felt disappointed — really disappointed. But was I going to let bitterness take root?

Sighing, I grabbed hold of God's grace and tried to figure out a way I could participate. I glanced out the living room window and noticed a planter with nothing in it. It looks pretty drab, I thought. I'll bet my friends would appreciate a couple of geraniums. I drove to a nursery, got one of the clerks to help, and then came back with a bag of soil and a few plants. It wasn't hard to find someone looking for an excuse to escape the paint fumes inside and eager to do some planting. Soon the red geraniums were potted to welcome the new tenants.

We make little choices for grace every day. Because every day, stuff happens. Your friend shows up late for the car pool. The bag boy drops your eggs. A friend forgets to say thank-you for the gift you gave him. Your neighbor's dog leaves his calling card on your front lawn. How do you respond?

Perhaps today you are pressed up against one of those choices. Take hold of Hebrews 12:15. Choose grace. It's always the better way. *Help me, Father God, to release bitterness. Then enable me to grab on to grace — for my sake and for those around me.*

It's difficult to describe how God can transform a moment — or a life — by the power of His grace. Sometimes, it's almost breathtaking.

A Picture of Grace

When the world sees us operating in the realm of grace, they must pause to wonder how and why. But the real answer, as I've said, is neither how nor why. It is Who.

It was talent night at one of our Joni and Friends family retreats, and Cindy, a young woman with severe cerebral palsy, was the last one scheduled to perform. Cindy's mother pushed her daughter in her wheelchair out onto the platform. Cindy, she told us, had been working hard all week on her song, "Amazing Grace."

Several of us looked at each other. We all loved Cindy, but how was this going to work? Because of her disability, Cindy couldn't speak.

Then her mother walked offstage and left Cindy alone. The young woman laboriously stretched out her twisted fingers and pushed a button on her communication device attached to her chair. And out came the monotone computerized voice, *Amazing grace, how sweet the sound, that saved a wretch like me. . . .*

As the robotic voice continued the hymn, Cindy turned her head to face us, the audience, and with enormous effort, began to mouth all the words as best she could. What's more, her smile lit up the entire place.

It was a performance that any opera star or recording artist would envy. To be honest, I have never seen anything to equal it. "Amazing Grace" is not a new song, but that night, it was sung in an entirely new way. Although Cindy was unable to sing the words with her vocal chords, something happened as she leaned hard on Jesus and mouthed those words.

I can't explain how, but somehow it rose up in that auditorium as a ringing hymn of praise to God. It was as though Cindy's song was backed by an eighty-piece orchestra. I can imagine the angels leaning over the edge of heaven, filled with wonder, to catch every word.

Live While You're Waiting

This morning when the aide came to put me on the gurney to go to Urology Lab, I was honest-to-goodness excited. I've been stuck in my room for what seems like ages now, waiting for the surgery on my pressure sore to heal. The idea of going anywhere, even to the other side of the hospital, sounded a whole lot better than biding time in my bed, looking out the window, or watching "The Price Is Right." New hallways to go down. New corners to turn. New rooms to look into as I pass by. New faces to see.

But I've been parked here outside of Urology for more than two hours now, and the novelty wore off long ago. I am tired of waiting. Tired of watching the clock above the door. It seems I'm always waiting. When I was at City Hospital, I waited to come here to Greenoaks. Once I got here, I waited to go to PT. At PT, I waited my turn for treatment. Once done, I waited for someone to push me back to my room.

I'm always waiting—for lunch, for dinner, for a visitor to come by, for my doctor to see me, and now … for a urology exam. I am so sick and tired of lying around and waiting. Is anything ever going to happen? Will it ever get better? Will I ever smile? Will I ever be able to quit waiting?!

FORTY-PLUS YEARS LATER

God, are You there?
Silence.
Are You listening?
More silence.
Ummm . . . am I getting the idea that You're asking me to wait? Is that what I'm supposed to do? Just—sit here and WAIT?
A very long silence.
Why is it, God, that when I want to charge ahead, You insist I wait? And at other times—when I feel like waiting—You push me forward?
Deafening silence.

You had hoped God wouldn't do this. Not now, not at this time, not in this situation. But He has, and it's exasperating. He replies to your questions with long, drawn-out periods of silence. No answers, no directions, no warm fuzzies, no whispers in the night, no road sign pointing, "This is the way, walk ye in it." Just . . . waiting.

Okay. If I have to sit here and wait, then I'll . . . I'll. . . .

Before you know it, you've created your own noise, activity, and excitement—anything but that grating stillness which seems to rub against the grain of your soul.

Oswald Chambers has observed, "When we are in an unhealthy state physically or emotionally, we always want thrills. And in the spiritual domain, if we insist on getting thrills . . . it will end in the destruction of spirituality."

But I'm tired of waiting! you say.

Ah, the Spirit of Christ hasn't forgotten you. He's listening. Finally you heave a deep sigh. *I'm at the end of my rope. I yield to You, Lord.*

And in that moment . . . the Spirit begins to work in your situation. Ignoring your frenzy and bypassing your busyness, God quietly elbows His way into your activity, whispering...

> *Be still, and know that I am God;*
> *I will be exalted among the nations,*
> *I will be exalted in the earth.*
>
> (Psalm 46:10)

Be Still

The Hebrew word God speaks here is *raphah.*

Can you hear it? Can you hear it in your agitation, anxiety, and worry? A friend of mine who was going through a period of deep anxiety — a season of his life when his stomach was tied in knots and his thoughts kept churning nonstop — thought he actually heard God speak this directly to his heart.

"It seemed like the words came from outside me," he explained, "cutting through that fog of worry and mental turmoil with the force of a command. I've never heard God speak so clearly to me — before or since."

What he heard so clearly were the words, *"Hush! Be still!"* Which is a pretty good English translation of *"Raphah!"*

The New American Standard Bible translates this term "Cease striving." Among the definitions for *raphah* are terms like "abate," "cease," "forsake," "leave," and "let alone." One commentator noted that *raphah* "means to let fall; to let hang down; then, to be relaxed, slackened, especially the hands: It is also employed in the sense of not making an effort; not putting forth exertion; and then would express the idea of leaving matters with God, or of being without anxiety about the issue."[4]

In contemporary lingo, we might hear someone say, "Oh, would you give it a rest?"

It's so very difficult in this era to find places and occasions that lend themselves to being still and setting aside our activities. And chances are, even if we found such places and times, we wouldn't like them! We're not used to it. Silence seems like something foreign, something alien to the world as we know it. In our cars, traveling from here to there, we flip on the CD player or tune in on the endless drone of talk radio. Or maybe we're doing the talk-talk-talking to people on our hands-free cell phone. When we're alone in the house, we turn the TV on even if we're not watching it — just to have some background noise. Just look around! So many people you see at airports or in shopping malls have tiny cell phones clipped to their ears or iPod ear buds tucked into ear canals.

"Be still and know that I am God"? How can we consider any such thing when we are never still?

May I suggest taking an hour — or even twenty minutes — to get outside and find that stillness in His creation today? You may not be near a desert or the mountains, but locate a place of quiet, a scene of icicle silence. A park covered in snow. A tree wearing icy diamonds in the sunlight. A distant woods across a field. Or perhaps a pink and orange sunset from your back porch. Take in the beauty around you ... then join in with the landscape and be still before God in wordless worship.

But the Lord's word here implies more than an absence of sound. It speaks of relaxing our convulsive grip on all the details of life, and placing our concerns, worries, fears, and burdens into the hands of God Himself. And then leaving them there!

I love David's words in Psalm 131. He says:

> *I do not concern myself with great matters*
>   *or things too wonderful for me.*
> *But I have stilled and quieted my soul;*
>   *like a weaned child with its mother,*
>   *like a weaned child is my soul within me.*

A child who hasn't been weaned frets and fusses for his mother's breast. But a weaned child is content to be close to his mother and rest quietly in her arms. David says, in effect, "I've forced myself to stop fretting about things I can't control or really do anything about. I've stopped trying to put everything together and figure everything out. I've given up trying to be a junior god in a miniature universe, and I'm going to still and quiet my troubled soul so that I can simply rest all these things in Your hands."

That is one of the best ways I can think of to know God in a deeper way.

To be still and ... wait.

I have learned that lesson from spending years in forced bed rest. Up in my wheelchair, I can at least flail my arms or shrug my shoulders. But on my bed, gravity works against me and, for that reason, I'm even more paralyzed when lying down.

And here is a ruby, hard-won. My enforced stillness has led me into a deeper firsthand knowledge of God through prayer.

It may only be seven o'clock in the evening when I'm put into bed, and I may not go to sleep until eleven. That leaves me with hours each day to still myself ... and pray. Sometimes I'm amazed that, from my bed, I can help set into motion the cogs and wheels of God's workings in the world. Through my prayers I may change the destiny of a life — or even a nation. Lying on my bed, I can hasten the day of the Lord's return. I don't move a muscle in those hours, but I help move the hand of God here and abroad.

My enforced stillness has led me into a deeper firsthand knowledge of God through prayer.

Here is how I begin each night. I settle my mind and my heart to become as still as my body (which may take a while!). In the quietness, I invite the Spirit of God to speak to me. I press my weakness up against His strength, my ignorance up against His knowledge, my fears and concerns up against His calmness and tranquility.

And we speak to one another in the stillness.

"An intercessor," says Hannah Hurnard, "means one who is in such vital contact with God and with his fellowmen that he is like a live wire closing the gap between the saving power of God and the sinful men who have been cut off from that power."[5]

Even though you have a hard time believing that any worthwhile activity can exist in stillness, God begins to do His hushed work in your heart.

- He gives you His inexplicable calm as you wait by the hospital bed of your husband.
- He gives you patience as you wait for the letter of acceptance from college.
- He grants you peace as you wait for the job opportunity.
- He draws alongside you to settle your agitated soul when you suffer from unrelenting pain.

And more than that, He gives you Himself, His intimacy as you search for a balm for your grief and answers to your deepest longings. It dawns on you that "rush" is wrong nearly every time.

It's a command; it's a charge: "Keep silence before me, ... and let the people renew their strength" (Isaiah 41:1 KJV).

It's a bidding, a mandate: "Be silent, all mankind, before the Lord" (Zechariah 2:13 TLB).

When we do, when we are, wonder of wonders! We hear "a still, small voice." God's answer comes only through waiting.

But It Isn't Easy

Most of my friends with disabilities would agree that one of the hardest disciplines any of us must grapple with is patience. It's one of those lessons we have to relearn every day, many times over.

On the mornings that Ken teaches, for instance, a friend comes to our house to do my morning routine and see me off to work. Often my friend will say something like "What a lovely day!"

Or "I don't think it's going to be nearly as hot today as it was yesterday."

When I hear comments like that, I want to bounce out of bed, head for the backyard, and appraise the day for myself. I want to breathe some of that fresh morning air. I want to see my roses while they're still covered with dew.

But it's simply not possible. I might as well wish to fly out the window like a little bird. My morning routine — including exercises and bathing — chews up an hour or more before I can even get into my wheelchair. So be patient, I must!

It's during such moments of waiting I think of all that has to be done. Do you identify with that? Sitting in the waiting room at the doctor's office you remember half a dozen phone calls you need to make. Parked in a long line of stop-and-go traffic on the freeway you think of all the stuff you need to pick up at the market on the way home — and the time is getting late.

It's a fact. Waiting is not an easy thing to do.

Unfortunately, most of us associate the word with phrases like "hanging around" or "killing time." We get a mental picture of leaning up against a wall with our arms folded, yawning, occasionally glancing at our watch.

But there's far more to waiting than lounging around until we receive what we hope for. George Matheson wrote insightfully about the *manner* in which we should wait.

We commonly associate patience with lying down. We think of it as the angel that guards the couch of the invalid. Yet there is a patience that I believe to be even more difficult — the patience that can run. To lie down in the time of grief, to be quiet under the stroke of adverse fortune, implies a great strength. But I know of something that implies a strength greater still. It is the power to work under stress, to continue under hardship, to have anguish in your spirit and still perform daily tasks.

This is a Christ-like thing. The hardest thing is that most

of us are called to exercise patience, not in the sick-bed, but in the street.

Waiting is something more than "counting flowers on the wall," as the old song goes. It takes *courage* to live out our patience on the street, to wait and yet still remain active and involved.

"Wait on the LORD," Psalm 27:14 tells us, "be of good courage, and He shall strengthen your heart; wait, I say, on the LORD!" (NKJV).

By implication, then, we can deduce that if we refuse to wait on Him, He will *not* bless us with "good courage" or strengthen our hearts. And our slide from anxiety to despair picks up speed.

Those times we find ourselves having to wait on others may be perfect opportunities to train ourselves to wait on the Lord. Instead of fidgeting and fuming, we could use such moments to pull Bible verses out of our memory, or learn more of God's Word.

I'm not talking about the mechanical repetition of words, but actually weaving biblical truth into the fabric of our day.

Wait on the Lord in prayer as you sit on the freeway, sharing with Him the anxiety of so many jobs to be done in such a short time. Watch your frustrations melt into praise as you sing hymns and choruses for His ears alone.

By exercising this kind of patience, rooted in God's Word, we can say with the psalmist, "I wait for the LORD, my soul waits, and in his word I put my hope" (Psalm 130:5).

Waiting for His Timing

Waiting for the Lord means putting His desires before our own, believing that He will meet our needs with generosity and love in His good time.

You may find yourself mightily tempted to do something on the spur of the moment. It may be an important decision. A desire you want gratified. A choice you don't feel like putting off. Or something you just want *now*.

Your itchiness to have things your way has you ready to settle for something of lower quality or less value. It could be a special purchase. Or a choice in jobs. Or a relationship. It could be a crossroads in your ministry. And the truth is—you really don't *want* to check in with the Lord, discern His mind and His desires, and wait for His green light.

Ah, but while we may regret a hasty decision a million times over, we will never regret waiting for the Lord. You can never go wrong as you wait and pray and still yourself in His presence, seeking His mind and heart.

He will end up giving you something better.

He will give you rubies of wisdom you couldn't obtain any other way.

And He will give you Himself.

When you have apprehended Him in a new, fresh way, it will all become clear. The choice will be obvious. The waiting will be worth it.

What you might provide for yourself by your effort, in your wisdom, and in your timing *cannot be compared* to what God has for you in His plan and in His timing.

Are you at a crossroads of decision in your life? Are you dealing with a desire that's pushing you to hurry? *Fight, fight, fight* the temptation to run ahead of Him. Lay your desires and petitions at His feet, and wait for His peace.

So...

if you're single and waiting for marriage...

if you're a preteen and waiting for high school...

if you're stuck in your career and waiting for a break...

if you're parked in a wheelchair and waiting for a push...

if you're married and waiting for your husband to change...

keep your head held high and place all your expectations in the Lord, rather than in uncertain, changeable circumstances.

Here is another ruby—hard-won wisdom the Lord has given me after four decades in a wheelchair. We don't wait to live. We have to keep living *while* we're waiting.

It takes courage to wait patiently and yet get out there and embrace life. But you can do it. Lean on God and courage will never be in short supply.

We don't wait to live. We have to keep living while we're waiting.

I remember a telephone call from several years ago that reminds me of "giving God time." The call came into the counseling department of the Dutch Christian Television Network. "I am a quadriplegic," the caller said. "I had said I would kill myself in ten years if I could not find help. It is now the tenth year. This is my only hope."

The young man had called in response to one of my programs on TV in the Netherlands. He had heard my message of hope and trusted that somehow people could respond to his needs. Contacts were made, help organized, and now we wait for God to heal the young man's heart.

We were all saddened and shocked by this story. It was hard to imagine no one being able to help this person and give him relief these past *ten years*. But what was just as shocking to me was the man's patience. He gave himself (and God) ten years! Most people in his situation rarely take such a long-term view of their circumstances. They want relief and they want it now.

The discouraged people that grab God's attention are those who intentionally set out to wait. Like the psalmist, they know it may take a while. They not only wait; they watch. They watch because they know that God will answer. Rather than standing on a street corner of life, waiting for God, they go about their days unencumbered. They are productive, joyful people, knowing that God will come in due time.

Wait. Wait patiently and eagerly. But in the meantime get busy with what you know to be your responsibilities.

Continue to live while you are waiting.

Waiting in Prayer

When our *Wheels for the World* team was in Peru, we met Angelica Ramirez, a twenty-five-year-old woman who had cerebral palsy and epilepsy since birth. For most of her life, she had laid in bed all day—her only entertainment was watching a shaft of sun move across her room. On the morning of our wheelchair distribution, Angelica's mother wrapped her daughter in a white mattress so her brother could carry her down the mountain. They were hoping to receive a wheelchair.

Our team happened to have a recliner wheelchair with an extended headrest (we don't usually take these sorts of highly customized chairs on trips). As Angelica was placed in this particular chair, everyone gasped. It fit *perfectly*. When our team gave Angelica's mother a Bible in the Spanish language, she broke down and began sobbing. "God has answered my prayer!" she said through an interpreter.

We smiled, thinking she meant the Bible. But the woman shook her head and explained, "I want you to understand that I have been praying twenty years for a wheelchair for my daughter and today—*Gloria al Dios*—God has answered my plea. Now I can take my daughter to church. I won't have to worry about carrying her!"

Twenty years?

If God answers your prayer immediately, be thankful; if it's denied, be patient; if you are to wait, remain eager and expectant. Angelica's story taught me something fresh about laying our requests before God: He invites us to have an expectant attitude when we pray. He wants us to be hopeful and eager—even if the answer is delayed for twenty years! Why such a delay? Only God knows, but I know this: He provided a perfect wheelchair hand-tailored for Angelica, and that Peruvian mother experienced twenty times the joy.

Strength While You Wait

Years ago my family and I took a camping trip up into the nature reserve of Jasper Provincial Park in Alberta, Canada. I remember boarding a chairlift that cabled us to the top of a huge glacier-scarred mountain overlooking a broad expanse of pine forest below. There our eyes met the spectacle of wild, rugged terrain and turquoise lakes shimmering in the sun. We shivered inside our down jackets, half from the icy cold and half from the awesome view. We yelled our delight to one another over the violent roaring of the wind at the mountaintop.

I marveled at the sight of a soaring eagle moving far across the wooded valley. Just a tiny speck against the distant mountain range. I watched as the eagle circled and dived, admiring his grace and ease.

Eagles seem to go with big things—mountains, canyons, great depths, immense heights. It's always at the most stupendous and alluring spectacles of nature that we find them.

God talks about eagles. In one of the most well-loved passages of the Old Testament, He uses their flight to describe the adventure that will unfold to the suffering Christian who waits for Him.

> *Though youths grow weary and tired,*
> *And vigorous young men stumble badly,*
> *Yet those who wait for the LORD*
> *Will gain new strength;*
> *They will mount up with wings like eagles,*
> *They will run and not get tired,*
> *They will walk and not become weary.*
> (Isaiah 40:30–31 NASB)

Does this sound like wearisome waiting to you? Does this sound like "shooting half the day before real action begins"?

Think of a really good waiter in an excellent restaurant. What does it mean that he "waits on you"? It certainly isn't a laid-back, ho-hum affair. Not if he wants a tip! A first-rate waiter will be quick to respond to your call and diligent to "check in on you" during the course of the meal to make sure you're enjoying it and have everything that you desire. That's active waiting. And that's how we should wait on God.

Good morning, Lord, is there anything I can do for You this morning?

Is there anything I can bring to You to meet any of Your desires?

Can I serve You in some special way this day?

Thinking back to that famous eagle passage in Isaiah 40 — it's not as though we *first* wait and *then* finally get the chance to mount up with wings, run without tiring, and walk without weariness. No, those good things actually happen *while* we are waiting! Waiting on God is an active, confident trusting — an instant obedience.

Isaiah promises a new and exciting perspective when we wait on the Lord. Waiting on God gives us the kind of perspective that an eagle must have who mounts up above the trees, lakes, and mountains. Our surroundings come into focus. Our horizons are broadened. We see our place in the scheme of things.

When the Bible talks about waiting on God in my suffering, it means confidently trusting that God knows how much I need and can take. It means looking expectantly toward the time when He will free me from my burdens.

But not get weary? Not get tired or stumble?

How can that be when these are the very trademarks of those who suffer? Yet God's promise is clear. Those who wait for Him in their distress will receive strength and endurance which others know nothing about.

Because I know that one day I'll receive a new body, I am now "able to mount up with wings like an eagle." It is my hope that makes me soar. It is my expectancy and anticipation that give me endurance and strength.

My body is now held by the limits of this wheelchair. But the waiting hope I have in God's future for me gives me the freedom to soar to heights of joy and explore the canyon depths of God's tender mercies.

All in all, it's worth the wait.

> *But you must return to your God;*
> *maintain love and justice,*
> *and wait for your God always.*
>
> (Hosea 12:6)

Creation Waits

In significant ways, mostly beyond our understanding, Creation itself is waiting.

Romans 8:19 tells us that "The creation waits in eager expectation for the sons of God to be revealed." J. B. Phillips renders it like this: "The whole creation is on tiptoe to see the wonderful sight of the sons of God coming into their own."

On tiptoe! . . . In some mysterious way, the flowers and plants and animals and seascapes and landscapes wait with excited expectancy for a glory yet to be revealed. Paul tells a little more about this anticipation.

> The world of creation cannot as yet see reality, not because it chooses to be blind, but because in God's purpose it has been so limited—yet it has been given hope. And the hope is that in the end the whole of created life will be rescued from the tyranny of change and decay, and have its share in that magnificent liberty which can only belong to the children of God!
> (Romans 8:20–21 Phillips)

One day the earth will be liberated. The whole creation, like us, is "groaning as in the pains of childbirth right up to the present time" (Romans 8:22). I sense this whenever I see smog, a junkyard, a forest that's been clear-cut and not replanted, or even a dead raccoon on the road.

When I drive the coastal mountains just a stone's throw from my home and marvel at the jutted, jagged rocks and canyons, I'm vividly aware I'm in the middle of earthquake country. Mud slides and aftershock happen all the time around here. These hills are restless.

Even though this little jewel of a blue planet has been scarred and denuded, abused and polluted, it will not be abandoned.

God doesn't waste things. He redeems them.

This passage in Romans 8 reveals the Lord's intentions for this blue marble of His. The earth upon which we trod is the earth that Christ will bring into His glorious freedom.

Something's coming ... something better.

If you want to know what this something is, study Revelation and Isaiah. "The wolf will live with the lamb" (Isaiah 11:6), and "the burning sand will become a pool" (Isaiah 35:7). We will have a part in liberating the new earth—perhaps uplifting the poor of Kurdistan, reforesting the hills of Lebanon, or planting trees along the Amazon. We may clear the slums of Rio de Janeiro, get rid of nuclear waste, and teach the nations how to worship God and how to beat their swords into plowshares.

God won't abandon the earth. He will redeem it.

The creation is groaning and longing for the day when God will release it from its bondage and usher in a new era with Christ as King.

Have you ever been out in nature and sensed something ... almost wistful? God's handiwork in mountains, seas, skies, and forests is mind-boggling. But the Bible tells us that—as lovely and amazing as our world may be—we do not live in the creation God originally intended. When, as a result of man's rebellion and sin, the curse of God fell like a shadow across our world, much that was wondrous, delightful, beautiful, and fairly shimmering with potential and possibility has fallen into bondage.

But it will not always be so.

Can you hear the sighing in the wind?

Can you feel the heavy silence in the mountains?

Can you sense the restless longing in the sea?

Something's coming ... something better.

But consider this: if the creation has an earnest expectation, surely we believers—the sons and daughters of God—should have nothing less! If the whole inanimate and brute creation is eagerly expecting, earnestly looking forward to the appearing of Jesus and all that means, the same kind of hope should be much more evident in you and me.

Watchman on the Wall

What do you think of when you think of "eager expectation"? The psalmist tried to express it with a simple word picture.

> *I wait for the LORD, my soul waits,*
> *and in his word I put my hope.*
> *My soul waits for the Lord*
> *more than watchmen wait for the morning,*
> *more than watchmen wait for the morning.*
> (Psalm 130:5–6)

Picture a lonely, middle-aged sentry on night duty, pacing back and forth on the top of Jerusalem's wall, as the long hours drag on. His feet are tired, his back aches, and the cold night air has seeped into his bones. There's no one to talk to, nothing stirring, and no sound but a chilly wind whistling along the stone parapets.

With no real way of marking the passage of time, those dark hours seem endless. After his hundredth revolution around the wall, he begins to glance toward the east—but it's just as black and star-strewn as the sky in the west. Back and forth, up and down, round and round, his sandals make a soft crunching noise as he paces.

And on every trip around the walls, he looks toward the east. Could the stars be fading just a bit along the horizon? Could there be just the slightest hint of gray? Is it his imagination, or did he hear a songbird in the date palms far below? *Won't morning ever come?*

What have you waited for with eager expectation? What sets your heart to yearning?

A pregnancy and a child to hold in your arms?

A letter from a sweetheart in a distant city?

A day when you can walk away from a tedious job and retire with a boat and a fishing pole?

Christmas morning when you were a child, and the chance to tear open those beautiful, mysterious gift boxes under the tree?

An all-clear result from a CT scan looking for recurrent cancer?

Your first solo flight in a private plane?

An end to a long military tour of duty in a faraway place and a plane ticket home?

A friend of mine remembers spending a few childhood days with a young cousin at his grandparents' house out in the country. Both of them became homesick, but the little cousin most of all. On the day his parents and family were to return for him, he sat in his grandfather's rocking chair by the big picture window in the living room ... just rocking back and forth and staring at the gravel road out in front of the house.

When his grandfather passed by several times and saw him sit-ting there, still as a stone, gazing intently at the gravel road winding into the distance, he said to the little boy, "Bill, I swear, you're going to look a hole right through that window."

Little Bill was on tiptoes waiting for that familiar 1954 blue-and-white Ford station wagon to come rolling along that country road in a cloud of dust. The Bible says that we too should wait "on tiptoes" for the day when Jesus returns for His own, calling us to heaven, and when He finally returns to earth to set things right. Do you find yourself longing and looking forward to the glorious appearing of the Lord Jesus Christ?

We mustn't wait in a dull sort of way with an indifferent attitude. We must rejoice in our hope — in spite of our suffering, in the face of whatever difficult life circumstances we may be enduring. It's that joy that makes you eagerly expect — like a big St. Bernard when he strains at his leash. Anticipation means stretching our necks. Yearning. Fervently hoping.

If that's the sort of attitude that nature has about the coming of that great day, you and I can learn a thing or two from the creation around us. Next time when you see a ray of sunlight suddenly pierce through a heavy, dark, afternoon sky, think about Romans 8:19.

If nature waits on tiptoe for the coming of Jesus, you and I shouldn't be caught flat-footed!

6

A Legacy of Prayer

I tried to pray this morning. I *needed* to pray. But the words just weren't there. I couldn't think. Was it because of the injury? The medications? I don't know. I don't know. I felt like someone in a little canoe out on a lake in a heavy fog. I would paddle first one way and then another, but I could never seem to go in a straight line or get any closer to shore. Everything seemed muffled and strange, and I couldn't see any landmarks to guide me.

And then I just got tired of paddling. Tired of even trying.

So instead of reaching for words that wouldn't come, I just started thinking about Jesus: Walking the earth doing miracles. Touching the man at Bethesda. Holding the little children in His lap. Hanging on the cross. And now, lifted up so high. Beautiful, like the morning star just before sunrise.

That's when it hit me. Jesus was *with* me in that canoe, out in the fog. My landmark wasn't out there somewhere, He was in the boat. And I didn't need to talk just then. I could rest, feeling Him close, knowing He was there.

FORTY YEARS LATER

That's not all bad.

The fact is, there are still times in my life when words flee from me. I want to pray. I want to be near to God. But because of pain or heaviness of spirit, I can't summon the energy to put a prayer together.

I'm reminded of a little poem from one of my favorite books.

> *Prayer is the burden of a sigh,*
> *the falling of a tear;*
> *the upward glancing of an eye,*
> *when none but God is near.*

My friend Margaret Clarkson, now with the Lord, penned those words. And that bit of verse summarizes so much of what I learned from this godly woman.

Margaret was a missionary in Canada who wrote many wonderful poems — and virtually each one was born out of her life of severe and chronic physical pain. The last time I was with Margaret was at Ontario Bible College. We spent lunchtime together talking, me in my wheelchair, and she lying on her side on a cot. She was in so much pain she simply could not stand up for any length of time. As a result, Margaret taught me many lessons about praying through pain.

I'm sure you can understand. You've probably experienced aching, sleepless nights when prayer seems impossible, when you simply cannot summon up enough physical or mental energy to put two sentences together in prayer — let alone pray to God "in His own language," as I've suggested.

Or perhaps you wake up to face another day of watching a suffering loved one — and you are utterly exhausted and completely unable to gather the shreds of your shattered personality and bring your unspeakable need before the throne.

Margaret Clarkson experienced many a painful time like this, and I'll never forget when she said, "Joni, the first thing we must realize is that it is neglect of prayer or refusal to pray that is sin, not the inability to pray. If the earnest desire to pray is present, we must not condemn ourselves because we find prayer hard or even impossible."

Looking back, I believe my missionary friend was harkening back to Psalm 38 where the psalmist cries, "LORD, all my desire is before You; and my sighing is not hidden from You" (Psalm 38:9 NKJV). And elsewhere it says, "The desire of our soul is for Your name and for the remembrance of You" (Isaiah 26:8 NKJV).

That was true of my friend Margaret. Her struggle to pray was never out of neglect or refusal. It was simply at times her inability to order her prayers before the Lord in a clear and concise way.

But that didn't really matter, because she never really stopped communicating with God. She offered Him her groanings.

And because of that, God fulfilled the desire of this extraordinary woman who truly feared the Lord. Yet this dear saint waged a never-ceasing warfare against allowing her infirmity to gain the place of power in her life, a warfare against allowing her physical pain to come between her and Jesus.

If you are in pain—or perhaps gripped with grief or anxiety—as you read these words, you may find prayer a difficult proposition. What you do manage to whisper to God seems feeble and faint.

Maybe so. But that fact doesn't change the reality of Psalm 145:18:

> *The LORD is near to all who call on him,*
> *to all who call on him in truth.*

Jesus stands at the right hand of God's throne on your behalf, and He is touched with the feeling of your infirmities. Are your prayers faint and weak? Take heart. Jesus is praying for you.

And never, never underestimate the ability of our God to use the shakiest prayer of the weakest saint to move heaven and earth.

Maybe something like the prayers of Corrie ten Boom, in her final days.

Praying in the Spirit

Corrie ten Boom survived the Nazi concentration camps and went on to travel the world to share Christ with millions. A series of strokes severely incapacitated her, after which she retreated to the sanctuary of her small home in southern California. But Corrie's ministry did not stop. Her house became a sanctuary of prayer.

Shortly before Jesus took her home, I went to visit with her. I wheeled into Tante Corrie's house, and the air was fragrant with the aroma of European coffee. A clock ticked and a kettle whistled. I sat in her parlor, enjoying old photographs of the ten Boom family while I waited for Pam, her helper, to wheel Corrie out of her bedroom. When she arrived, we talked—actually I did most of the talking, since the strokes had severely limited her speech. I also sang to her several favorite hymns. What a grand visit!

Before I left, Corrie grasped her paralyzed hand with her good hand. Then, with great effort, entwined the fingers. Pam, understanding this gesture, knelt by Corrie's wheelchair and looked up into that determined face.

"Tante Corrie, may we pray with you too?"

We bowed our heads and Corrie began. Her words were indistinct —part Dutch, part English, and part neither one—but her voice was strong as she prayed earnestly in the Spirit. The Spirit was, in fact, the only one who could understand her.

God could understand Corrie's seemingly jumbled intercession as clearly as He read Margaret Clarkson's heaven-directed sighs and groans. Romans 8:26–27 says,

> In the same way, the Spirit helps us in our weakness. We do
> not know what we ought to pray for, but the Spirit himself inter-

cedes for us with groans that words cannot express. And he who searches our hearts knows the mind of the Spirit, because the Spirit intercedes for the saints in accordance with God's will.

Don't try to diagram the path of these prayers in the Spirit or wrap a precise theological definition around them. Just know that God knows our every thought, and He has no difficulty sorting out English from Dutch from some deep well of spiritual language that could never be translated this side of heaven.

Margaret's quick thought in His direction through a searing wall of pain spoke volumes in heaven. And Corrie's apparent gibberish —Spirit-aided as it was—may have stopped angels in their tracks as it came before the Father.

But there is so much more to this mystery of prayer beyond even these wonders. And it shouldn't surprise us that rubies of surpassing value may be hard-won through suffering.

The Math of Heaven

Sometimes when my wheelchair gets me down or I feel like giving up because of the encroaching pain of paralysis, I think of a young woman named Kim, and I am encouraged to persevere.

Perhaps more than any other person, Kim showed me that my life—and your life—counts. And it counts more than we can possibly imagine.

I first learned about Kim when an elder from her church in Pennsylvania called to ask if I could contact her with a few words of encouragement. "Kim is a brilliant twenty-six-year-old Christian woman who has always been active in our church," he explained. "But last year she contracted motor-neuron disease and now must stay in bed. She can hardly move and must be fed with a feeding tube." The elder paused a moment, then added, "Kim is very depressed. She's wondering if her life is worth living anymore."

I telephoned Kim right away. Her mother tucked the receiver against her ear and against the pillow. I could hardly hear Kim's voice, her breathing was so faint. We discussed many things, including our favorite parts of the Bible, the subject of heaven, and prayer. Finally, Kim said faintly and with great labor, "Joni, they want to give me a ventilator to help me breathe, but I don't know whether I want one. I'm so tired. Do you think I should go on a ventilator?"

For a moment, I was speechless. Finally I took a deep breath, whispered a quick prayer, and replied, "Kim, there are a lot of things to consider—not the least of which is that your decision will affect many people around you. But of the two choices facing you, I think there's a better one." I then proceeded to tell her about a simple but powerful Bible verse that has encouraged and guided me through the toughest times of my forty-plus years of quadriplegia.

> Do not forget this one thing, dear friends: With the Lord, a day is like a thousand years, and a thousand years are like a day. (2 Peter 3:8)

We all know the old adage that God looks at the last two thousand years as only a couple of days gone by. But what about the other half of that verse? The part about seeing each day as a thousand years?

What kind of math is that?

It's the math of One who lives outside of time, is not bound by time, and can step in and out of time whenever He pleases to accomplish His purposes. If we really come to grips with the fact that God can pick up any twenty-four-hour day He chooses and give it an eternal impact of a thousand years, then each day of our lives becomes immeasurably important—and brimming with opportunity. Each day God gives us precious hours to invest in the lives of others—investments which will have eternal repercussions in our lives *and* theirs.

But let's carry the math out just a bit further. If twenty-four hours can have the impact of a thousand years, then what kind of impact could a single hour have?

I figure about forty-one and a half years.

And then what about a single minute?

Maybe something like eight and a half months.

Kim perked up as I began to speak with her about these thoughts. "But I'm in bed," she reminded me. "I can't go anywhere or do anything. How can my life count in this condition?"

"First, Kim," I replied, "you can pray. No matter how feeble or fainthearted your prayers may seem to you, they have a very special power with God. It says in Psalm 10:17, 'You hear, O LORD, the desire of the afflicted; you encourage them, and you listen to their cry.'

"Do you realize what this means, Kim? It means that the Lord cups His ear to listen when someone like you prays out of great affliction. He bends over backward when people offer Him a sacrifice of praise. Please hear me, Kim. I mean this with all my heart. God will *use* your intercessions to shake the lives of those around you ... as well as the destiny of *nations*."

It was a big, big thought for Kim, but it intrigued her.

"Your obedience, Kim, counts for eternity. Now is your chance to stretch your soul's capacity for God! Your patience and longsuffering and endurance will resound with more glory to God than you can possibly appreciate right now. As it says in Romans 8:18, 'I consider that our present sufferings are not worth comparing with the glory that will be revealed in us.' If you can hang in there and keep a godly response, then who can measure the impact? Who can put a value on how God will work through your prayers?"

Kim's body was feeble. Dying. But there was nothing weak or faint about her opportunities to do battle in the spiritual realm. I couldn't help but think of those beaten-up, battered believers described in the book of Hebrews "who through faith conquered kingdoms, administered justice, ... shut the mouths of lions, quenched the fury of the flames, and ... whose weakness was turned to strength" (Hebrews 11:33, 34).

Kim laughed as I went on and on. It was sweet to hear.

But that's the way this young woman chose to live out her days. Can any of us calculate the impact of her prayers? If she were to live only two more weeks with a perspective like this, that figures out to be fourteen thousand years' worth of eternal reward and glory. As she became progressively weaker and weaker, who is to say that her ministry in time and eternity didn't become stronger and stronger?

Unseen Realities

The lesson of 2 Peter 3:8 isn't only for Kim, it's for all of us who believe in the might of God and the power of prayer.

Archimedes of Syracuse was a Greek mathematician, physicist, astronomer, and engineer in the second century before Christ. Speaking of the lifting power of a lever, it was he who said, "Give me a lever long enough and a fulcrum on which to place it, and I shall move the world."

Presumably, even one tiny tap on that cosmic-sized device would move the whole planet. Prayer is like that giant lever. Our smallest efforts, in faith, can have results that stagger the imagination. Your prayers — even the smallest, weakest little gasps — can move nations and shape the destinies of multiplied thousands.

Little wonder that Psalm 90:12 has us praying to God, "Teach us to number our days aright, that we may gain a heart of wisdom." So value your days and make the most of every opportunity for doing good because *this* is the kind of wisdom God wants you to apply to your twenty-four-hour slices of time.

Life is so short, whether we're hale and hearty or severely disabled.

James 4:14 warns us, "What is your life? You are a mist that appears for a little while and then vanishes." No wonder the Bible describes each day as being like a thousand years—that's how price-less and precious they are! Life is fleeting, and of all the things we waste, let's not waste our sufferings.

I should tell you that Kim ended up living another month and a half after our conversation on the phone. But as her mother told me later on, those forty-five days—she looked at them as forty-five thousand years—were some of the most meaningful and important weeks she had ever lived. Her life demonstrates that we can all get a head start on eternity by understanding—and investing in—the real connection between this world and the next. Our prayers—as well as our obedience, sacrifices, and Christian encouragements to-ward others—have a direct and positive bearing on your capacity for joy, worship, and service to God in heaven.

Here is a statement that probably goes directly against the grain of anything you've ever heard from our contemporary culture: Life worth living is not found in a set of circumstances—whether pleas-ant or painful. Life worth living is found in a Person, the Prince of Life. The Resurrection and the Life. Jesus is the Way, the Truth, and the Life. He has the words of life. And the moments we invest in praying for His will to be done in lives, communities, and even nations will extend beyond this life—and beyond time itself.

Does this mean that every one of our prayers will be answered with a yes? No, but the prayers will be answered in a way that brings God the most glory—and ultimate good to our lives.

Mary and Martha must have felt perplexed—and personally devastated—when Jesus deliberately delayed coming to Bethany after He received news of Lazarus's illness: Why is the Master ig-noring our request? Doesn't He care about our brother? Surely He's forgotten about us.

The Bible tells us that Jesus heard the request and chose not to respond—at first. That divine decision made life hard for Mary and Martha in that brief season of time. Yet it is usually strange answers to prayer that hide the deepest, best, and most beautiful purposes.

Mary and Martha did not receive a brother healed from the infirmary; they received their brother raised from the cemetery. More than that, they received the gift of greater, sturdier, more robust faith. God is interested in the same for you.

God hasn't promised me happy endings to every life situation, but He has assured me of greater faith.

Here is a ruby, hard-won through forty years in a wheelchair: God hasn't promised me happy endings to every life situation, but He has assured me of greater faith. And that's the *best* ending, anyway.

The Legacy of Mary Rose

Just minutes before I was called up to the platform to address an overflowing convention several years ago, I met Mary Rose. She shuffled toward me, leaning on the arm of her escort, her gait stiff and her arm curled against her chest. I guessed she had cerebral palsy. She wore a tan cardigan over a yellow cotton dress. Nothing fancy. Her glasses sat askew on her nose.

"Joni," her escort said, "this is my friend Mary Rose, and she's been waiting so long to meet you."

Mary Rose stretched out her rigid arm to greet me. Her body may have been stiff, but her smile was warm. She was excited to meet me, the person who had written the book that had meant so much to her decades earlier. "And Joni," her escort said, "Mary Rose has something to tell you."

"I-have-been-pray-ing-for-you-ev-ery-day," she said with great effort, "ev-er-since-I-read-your-book."

Praying for me? *Every day?* I did some quick math in my head. Seven thousand times this woman has lifted me up to the Savior! I watched her shuffle away, back into the shadows, as I wheeled out into the light and the applause. But I didn't feel important at that moment. God isn't impressed by my books, paintings, speeches, and world travel. When it comes to "entering the Master's happiness," the highest accolades will go to people who have labored secretly and loyally in a daily—sometimes hourly—ministry of prayer.

Someday on the Other Side, when Mary Rose steps into the radiant light to receive her magnificent reward, I'll stand happily on the sidelines, cheering and applauding.

Those who have fought battles and conquered kingdoms in the secret places of prayer may never be recognized or affirmed in this life. But Someone has noticed every moment of that investment. And their reward will have nothing to do with being bigger or better, well-known or watched, attractive or charming.

But it will have everything to do with faithfulness.

7

Hope beyond Answers

Diana came in again today to read to me from the Bible.

She said, "Is there any special verse you want to hear, Joni?"

She asked, but she already knew.

It's the same every time she — or anyone else — comes in. I heard her little sigh. She wants me to pick something else. Maybe a couple of psalms. But I can't. I can't get enough of it.

It's a page in the Bible I've rehearsed over and over — through the long, boring parts of the day and the hours of endless night. It's about a place where I go in my mind. A place far, far from this hospital.

I moved my lips as Diana read. I have this part almost memorized.

Now there is in Jerusalem by the Sheep Gate a pool, which is called in Hebrew, Bethesda, having five porches. In these lay a great multitude of sick people, blind, lame, paralyzed, waiting for the moving of the water. For an angel went down at a certain time into the pool and stirred up the water; then whoever stepped in first, after the stirring of the water, was made well of whatever disease he had. Now a certain man was there who

117

had an infirmity thirty-eight years. When Jesus saw him lying there, and knew that he already had been in that condition a long time, He said to him, "Do you want to be made well?"

The sick man answered Him, "Sir, I have no man to put me into the pool when the water is stirred up; but while I am coming, another steps down before me."

Jesus said to him, "Rise, take up your bed and walk." And immediately the man was made well, took up his bed, and walked. (John 5:2–9 NKJV)

Diana closed the Bible, lowered her eyes. She didn't know what to say. Nobody ever knows what to say. But that doesn't matter. I don't really care. If someone wants to read to me — if they want to take time to sit by my bed and give me words from the Bible — that's what I want to hear.

Bethesda. I can see it all. Hear it. Feel it. Smell it. It has become like a movie in my mind, running in a continuous loop. Sometimes I'm "there" as much as I'm "here." In fact, I'm there right now....

It's Judea, two thousand years ago, at the Pool of Bethesda, with its sun-baked pavement and colonnades.

Heat shimmers. Flies buzz. A donkey brays. Somewhere off in the distance (I can hear it so clearly) a dog keeps barking. But the crowd around me, normally languid in the afternoon heat, is restless. Murmuring, shuffling, expectant without knowing why. (But I know.)

I'm just one of those disabled people — sick, paralyzed, diseased — out here on the hot pavement. Unable to even swat flies. That's who I am now, and I'd better get used to it. I'm one of them. Some of us are slumped on the steps leading down to the pool. Others lean up against the colonnades, looking for a little shade from this heat.

Heat sends my blood pressure up. But I don't care. I wouldn't move from this place even if I could.

I'm one of the lucky ones today, lying on a mat against a cool, shady wall. Someone covered me with a rough cloak. That was kind.

But others treat me like a piece of dirt on the street, even kicking me or stepping on my legs. I guess I get the last laugh on them — I can't feel a thing.

The sun climbs higher and I'm hot even in this poor shade. I can feel the sweat trickle off my scalp into my eyes. I'm thirsty.

I hope Jesus comes soon. No one else knows He is coming. But I do.

Now ... it's late afternoon. Something ripples in the air that isn't wind. Over by the colonnades, movement. A stir. A shout. The crowd parting.

And there He is. *Jesus*. Stepping out of the shadows into brilliant sunlight. My heart pounds in my ears. It's Him. It's really Him. He's stopped and turned — saying some words to a small group. I can't hear. Now He's stooping, touching the eyes of the blind man who's been here forever. I can hear the crowd gasp — then silence — then cheering. He's been healed! He can see!

Jesus, come to me. I need healing too! Son of David, help me. I'm over here by the wall!

People are elbowing, jostling, crawling, dragging themselves, pressing in on Him, trying to get near. This is better than an angel stirring the waters. This is the Healer Himself. But I can't move, can't crawl. And who will drag a paralyzed girl into His path?

Jesus, it's me ... Joni! Don't forget me. Don't pass me by again. Please! I'm over here!

He's not looking at me. He's turned to someone else. I thought — this time — He would come. I thought He would see how much I need Him and come, touch me, heal me. But now, I guess He's moved on.

That's how this movie loop in my head always ends. Somehow, it spins off the reel and splices into something else — a visitor at the door, a nurse coming to take my blood pressure, an orderly to change the bedding. And I'm so, so disappointed.

But maybe next time. Next time someone reads me that Scrip-ture the movie will finish a different way. Jesus will hear me, look my way. He'll put His strong, carpenter's hands on my face, speak to me, and I'll feel a tingle in the tips of my fingers and toes. Warmth and strength will shoot through my limbs. Then He'll smile and say, "Joni, get up. You can walk now!"

Oh, God, it seems like ages since I've been in this hospital. Where are You? Do You see me at all? Why am I not getting better?

FORTY YEARS LATER

If I could speak to that younger self of mine in the Baltimore hospital, I would say, "Joni, you were right. You were looking in the right direction all along.

"That movie that played over and over in your mind ... I know the ending now. It's forty years later, and I know what happens. I've seen the movie, and I know how it turns out.

"Jesus didn't walk away from you. He didn't ignore the cry of your heart. He didn't close His eyes to your plight or close His heart to your suffering. He did hear. He did respond. He came to you.

"No, He didn't heal your physical wounds, and I know that is hard to bear. But Joni, He picked you up into His arms like a little lamb, and He has carried you close to His heart ever since. You were in His embrace then, as I am in His embrace now. He is carrying you, Joni" (see Isaiah 40:11).

Just a few years ago, I went back to the scene of my youthful dreams and longings. But this time I went in person. And in that place where I would so often hide as a frightened teenager, I found something.

A priceless ruby.

JERUSALEM, SEPTEMBER 1998

It was a dry, warm, and windy day in old Jerusalem.

Ken and I passed through the bazaar and found ourselves in a quieter, less congested part of the city.

Somehow, it was more than just sightseeing to me that day. I felt like God had something there for me. Something to see. Something to experience. Something He'd been waiting to tell me. I know His presence is every bit as real and near in California or Maryland as it is in Jerusalem. Even so ... I felt an anticipation in my heart that went beyond normal curiosity about an interesting tourist spot.

We slowly meandered toward the Sheep Gate. Looking off to our right, we saw the tops of the cedar trees bending in the breeze above the Temple Mount. Making our way to the left, we followed a stone path bordering a church built by Crusaders and leading through a small grove of olive trees.

A warm breeze rustled the branches, and flowers along the path bobbed. It was almost like the wind was whispering something to me, but I couldn't make out the words.

No one was around but us, and all was oddly quiet.

Suddenly, the path opened out into an acre or two of white stone ruins. A plaque on the guardrail read:

> Now there is in Jerusalem by the Sheep Gate a pool, which is called in Hebrew, Bethesda, having five porches. In these lay a great multitude of sick people, blind, lame, paralyzed, waiting for the moving of the water....

Bethesda.

I stared at the verse a long time before lifting my eyes to explore the crumbled colonnades. I had never been there before and yet ... I had. Times beyond number. Lying in the hospital, hearing the story, placing myself there in my imagination, in my grief, in my yearning to be healed. I had waited and waited for Jesus in that very place. And now, it was as if that intense longing had permeated these very stones.

The place was deserted, and the city sounds seemed muted and far away, the wind sighing among the ruins. Ken decided to amble down to see if he could find any water left in the cistern below.

I stayed by the plaque on the railing. Waiting. Expectant.

The Exchange

It wasn't only God's Son who walked the narrow dusty tracks and stone-paved alleyways in Israel and Jerusalem.

Abraham too had traversed the tiny country Ken and I explored that day. The Lord had told him, "Go, walk through the length and breadth of the land, for I am giving it to you" (Genesis 13:17).

And before Jerusalem was even Jerusalem, one who was known as a priest of God Most High and the king of Salem came out to meet the patriarch after his battles, bearing bread and wine (see Genesis 14:18–20).

I think about Abraham and Sarah, and how they had longed with everything in them for a child. God eventually granted them a son, just as He had promised, but before He gave them the desire of their hearts, He appeared to Abraham in a vision.

> *Do not be afraid, Abram.*
> *I am your shield,*
> *your very great reward.*
> (Genesis 15:1)

At the time, Abraham was too bound up by his fear and sorrow to respond to those magnificent words. He went on to say, "O Sovereign LORD, what can you give me since I remain childless....?" (Genesis 15:2).

I think God had just answered that question.

He was giving Abraham Himself.

He was the Prize. He Himself was the Very Great Reward. And if you have Him, if He has willingly given Himself to you in all His wonder, splendor, might, and love, what else do you need?

There's a ruby of wisdom in these thoughts, a flashing, many-faceted diamond of understanding. When God denies your dearest desire, get ready to open up your heart even wider, for He will become that desire Himself.

"I am ... your very great reward."

Abraham wasn't satisfied with God's answer, because his mind was locked on earthly things—a child, a son, an heir, a family. So often, in our troubles and human limitations, we're not satisfied either.

God understands, "For He Himself knows our frame; He is mindful that we are but dust" (Psalm 103:14 NASB). Even so, the Holy Spirit who dwells within us must long for a deeper understanding among God's children. If only

When God denies your dearest desire, get ready to open up your heart even wider, for He will become that desire Himself.

we could see with the eyes of faith just a little bit deeper into eternal realities. When we spurn God's offer of more of Himself in exchange for our cherished desires, it's a little like asking our dad for a nickel and being crushed with disappointment because he gives us all the gold in Fort Knox. The truth is, if God says no to one of our requests, it is only that He might say yes to something infinitely more valuable and beyond our reckoning.

Sometimes the process of weaning us from a lesser good in order to give us something much greater simply breaks our heart. The rich young ruler walked away sad after Jesus had offered him rewards in heaven and His own close companionship in exchange for his meager earthly portfolio. He just didn't understand. He just couldn't see. I wonder if, before he died, he ever did.

In the same way, you and I feel torn and grieve when our Christian loved one exchanges a brief, transitory, shadow life for life unending and the very presence of Christ just on the other side of death's door.

And as that young girl in the hospital bed in Baltimore forty years ago, I too was devastated when He declined to give me my heart's desire—a restored, whole, fully functional body.

Here is a ruby of wisdom, hard-won. It has taken me years to understand that what He has taken away in one currency He has given back—a million to one—in the currency of heaven.

By denying me the hope of physical healing, He has given me unspeakable privileges. Looking back, I am reminded that He has appointed me to be His ambassador of hope all over the world to so many who have no hope at all. I can close my eyes and see countless faces in over forty-five nations. Africa. Asia. Romania. The Middle East.

What He has taken away in one currency He has given back — a million to one — in the currency of heaven.

I think of *Wheels for the World*, and nearly forty thousand wheelchairs collected nationwide, refurbished by inmates in nineteen correctional facilities, and hand-delivered to needy disabled children and adults in poor, developing nations. I recall story after story of men and women and children who have been given hope—real, tangible, practical help—in forgotten places and desolate pockets of despair around the world. I think of the opportunity to declare the wonder and worth of Jesus to over a million listeners every week on my radio program. I think of hundreds and hundreds of special needs families that Joni and Friends will serve through our Family Retreats across the country.

And beyond all those opportunities to serve Him, to carry the hope of Christ around this dark world, He has given me Himself. He has told me, "Don't be afraid, Joni. I am your shield. I am your reward, your *very* great reward."

The Lord gives, the Lord takes away. And what He takes away may tear our hearts in two, but what He gives may change someone's world forever.

But let's be honest here. That "taking away" part can push us to the very brink.

Hope on the Edge

My friend David lives on the edge. He's a quadriplegic, his wife left him after the car accident, he survives on government benefits, and he lives alone in a little apartment downtown. After getting up in the morning he more or less fends for himself after his part-time attendant leaves. Despite all his struggles, David always orders the public access van on Saturday evening so that he can come to our church for Sunday services.

"Who helps you with dinner?" I asked him once. David explained that he usually powers his wheelchair over to the Pizza Hut. "The Lord always provides someone to help," he laughed. "Sometimes it's one of the waiters on break. Or a stranger having dinner who offers to help.

"I can feed myself," he said proudly. "I just need someone to place the pizza in the curve of my hand just so. But Joni, I'll tell you something, all this helps me to depend on the Lord. I mean.... I *depend* on Him."

Like flickering candles snuffed in the wind, this man's hopes had been extinguished one by one. Just try to imagine. Try to place yourself in his shoes.

The hope of marriage and lifelong love. Gone.

The hope of fathering sons and daughters. Gone.

The hope of rising to the top in a fruitful and engaging career. Gone.

And all of those incredibly precious little things in life. Peeling an apple. Fishing. Backpacking. Shooting a few baskets with the guys. Paddling a canoe across a still lake in the morning mist. Cooking dinner. Working out. Walking under the stars. All gone. All irretrievably out of reach for the rest of his life. With Job, he could have said,

> My *days have passed, my plans are shattered,*
>> *and so are the desires of my heart. . . .*
> *where then is my hope?*
> *Who can see any hope for me?*
>>>> (Job 17:11, 15)

David only has one — just one — answer to that question.
Jesus is David's only hope.
Literally.
David inspires me because he's not afraid to live on that edge.
Somehow he finds light in the darkness and hope in the midst of
helplessness. And God has revealed to him the preciousness of Isa-
iah 45:3 where the Lord promises,

> *I will give you the treasures of darkness,*
>> *riches stored in secret places,*
> *so that you may know that I am the LORD,*
>> *the God of Israel, who summons you by name.*

Out there on the frayed and tattered edge of life, David has
found a stash of rubies.
Oh, how wealthy are the people who need God desperately;
whose treasure in the darkness is a deeper knowledge of Him.

> *Blessed are you who hunger now,*
>> *for you shall be satisfied.*
> *Blessed are you who weep now,*
>> *for you shall laugh.*
>>>> (Luke 6:21 NASB)

In the midst of your own darkness, there are treasures, riches,
and rubies of wisdom that could never by discovered in the light
of ease and peace. Needing God desperately will *always* make you
wealthy.
But once again, arriving at that point may be the most difficult
path you can imagine.

A Choice of Life or Death

When someone is newly paralyzed, finding and holding on to such a hope can be the difference between life and death. If you become so depressed that you won't do physical therapy, won't get out of bed, or won't even eat, you've chosen the grave.

That's where Ron was. When his wife emailed me, the girls who help me with correspondence could immediately read the fear in her words.

"Joni," she wrote, "I'm so sorry to bother you. But would you please call my husband?"

A former pastor, Ron had broken his neck in a motorcycle accident and had been lying in bed for months. He had been sinking into such a profound depression that his wife became distraught. Her last straw was to "email Joni."

I talked on the phone to him for an hour, sharing Scriptures that had helped me through the dark times over the years. But Ron knew more Scripture than I did and simply refused to respond. I sang a few hymns to him, but I only got silence on the other end.

Finally, near the end of our time on the phone, I shot a quick prayer toward heaven and took a different tack.

"Ron, did you see the movie *The Shawshank Redemption?*" He seemed surprised at my question and indicated that he had.

"Maybe you remember Andy DuPhrane's line when he was talking to his fellow prisoner. He said, 'Hope is a good thing, maybe the best of things, and no good thing ever dies ... so get busy living, or get busy dying."

Ron was quiet for a long moment. Then he said softly, "Hope *is* a good thing." The former pastor returned to his hope in Christ. And from then on, he got busy living.

Titus 2:13 (KJV) speaks of, "Looking for that blessed hope, and the glorious appearing of the great God and our Savior Jesus Christ." From the Lord alone flows all joy and peace. With my own eyes, I saw hope overflow in Ron's life when he and his wife finally came to one of our Family Retreats. There they were, busy passing on hope to others!

All of this may sound good.

You might even think it sounds easy.

But we are speaking here about some of the deepest valleys and darkest nights of life. Times when you feel bumped up against the outer fence of your very sanity. Times when you wonder if you'll even survive. Times when you feel so weak and depleted or so locked in a vise of depression that you don't even have the strength or will to pray for help.

That was the case with my friend, Jeannie.

Hope in the Rock Higher than I

Jeannie asked me if I ever lose my handle on hope because of my pain or disability.

She has good reason to ask. Jeannie has been through monumentally difficult times over the last eighteen months. After a painful divorce, she gained a lot of weight, could *not* get it off, lost her job, and then developed a couple of medical problems related to her weight gain — which made finding a new job even *more* difficult.

She feels so alone sometimes. So crushed by hardships. She's not whining or looking for sympathy, but I can understand. Sometimes problems pile on so high they only seem to wear you down. She confided the other day that she didn't feel like she had the strength to even reach out for God.

"What do you do, Joni, when you feel hope slipping away from you?"

I don't always have something profound to say when I get asked a question like that. But the Scripture does. I've been rescued, I told her, more than many times by Psalm 61:2–3:

> *From the ends of the earth I call to you,*
>   *I call as my heart grows faint;*
>   *lead me to the rock that is higher than I.*

There are a couple of things I love about this verse. First, it doesn't matter if you are at the end of things—at the end of the earth—at the end of *yourself*, like my friend Jeannie. Please *know* that God will hear you.

"The ends of the earth" speaks of regions you would never willingly go. No one wants to look for an apartment on the backside of the moon. No one wants to pitch their tent in a wilderness of suffering. No one wants to linger along the road in the gray, twilight lands of depression. No one volunteers to walk that long, lonely highway of blasted hopes and demolished dreams.

We don't sign up to go such places. I never asked for paralysis. Jeannie never asked for betrayal and divorce. Nevertheless, whether we like it or not, our path in this life will traverse such places. Jesus *said* it would. At some point in the course of our lives, we will find ourselves at the ends of the earth.

Maybe so. But you are never so far down and out that God is not near.

The psalmist says he cried "as my heart grows faint" (Psalm 61:2 TNIV). The old King James Version says, "when my heart is overwhelmed." Psalm 61 is for anybody who has a fainting heart—that includes my friend, me, and you too. You know what it feels like to be overwhelmed. Your senses are numb, you feel spiritually tired, battered and bruised, your prayers don't seem to get answers, God seems far away, you feel like giving up, like throwing in the towel (or maybe like eating more chocolate, as my friend Jeannie has been prone to do).

If this describes you, friend, you've got a fainting heart!

But finally the psalmist cries, "Lead me to the rock that is higher than I." That thought amazes me. To me, it says that in those times when our hearts are so low and we feel so weak and depleted that we can't drag ourselves to that High Rock, we can ask the Rock to come to us. We can ask the Rock of Ages to take us by our weary hands and *lead* us to Himself.

Praise Him! When we're too weak and overwhelmed to come to Him, He will come to us!

And this is the way my friend finally sighed in the weakest of prayers, "Oh Lord, I have absolutely no strength. But I know enough to ask You to please, please inspire me, give me the 'want to,' give me the desire, Lord, to reach out to You. I need to get above things, I need a brighter, clearer outlook on things—and You, Lord Jesus, are the Rock that is higher than I am."

It's been a while since her husband left her, and Jeannie still has a few pounds to shed—she's doing that to get her health back. But things are looking up for my friend right now. And Psalm 61 and the grace of God which can be found in it—and in all of God's Word—is her rock.

Jeannie had come to me looking for answers.

But sometimes there simply aren't any answers to be found.

Hope beyond Answers

I couldn't think of a better way to spend time off in my hometown than to dress up for a fancy luncheon with my high school girlfriends and swap stories, pass photos, dig up funny memories, and carve out an hour for prayer and hymn singing. We hadn't been together since graduation in '67, and I was on pins and needles to see them.

"Hey Connie," I said to my friend over the phone, "I'm flying into Baltimore for a speaking engagement in a couple of weeks, and I would love to get together with some old Young Life club friends."

I wheeled through Connie's front door three weeks later, geared up for a soulful afternoon.

"What did you do to your hair?"

"Hey, I brought a couple of old songbooks."

It was a traffic jam of hugs and hellos in the entry way of her house until Connie called us into the dining room. Linen, china, bowls of fruit, and fresh flowers greeted us.

"Okay, I have only three requests," I announced after grace was sung and platters started around the table. "Set aside time for prayer, singing, and each give an update on what's been happening."

Millie, at the far end with her arm in a cast, started. Yes, we'd all sign her cast before leaving, and, yes, I promised I wouldn't drool when I autographed it with my mouth. No, we didn't realize it had been on for months. Oh really? The prognosis is that bleak? The news of chronic infection subdued us.

Next was Jacque, my fun-loving friend with whom I had shared boyfriends, milkshakes, and laps around the hockey field. "You all know about my husband. It didn't work out between us. My son's having a rough time...." She spoke to her plate, pushing food with her fork. The table was quiet except for the clinking of silverware.

The mother of my high school boyfriend, Mrs. Filbert, told how her son's wife had fled the marriage, leaving her to tend to her grandchildren while he worked. Now that the grandkids were older, she was devoting her time to her husband stricken with Parkinson's. I heard the words, but I saw memories of long-ago Friday evenings when I would play the piano in her stately home. A safe, orderly, beautiful home, which kept heartache beyond the threshold.

"Some people say I shouldn't give up speaking at Christian Women's Clubs," she said, her eyes becoming wet, "but I'm convinced the Lord has me where He wants me."

At the far end sat Diana, taking it all in. She hadn't said much. When we greeted each other, she seemed unusually quiet. It was her turn to speak. Diana's glum look fit her words as she shared a story of rebellion and drug abuse in her family. Dishes stopped clattering. Ever since high school, Diana had been a spiritual stalwart. Closer to God than any of us. It was she who read me the Bethesda story (over and over again) in my hospital room when I was seventeen.

But today, our immovable and unshakable Rock of Gibraltar stared into her lap. "I wasn't going to come to this luncheon. We brought my son home late last night from the rehab unit. It was pretty bad. I don't know … I just don't know."

Silence settled over us. One person felt uneasy with the quiet — Jacque, the one who had a son who was struggling. "Well you got to keep hoping, keep praying. Somehow, you got to know it's going to work out. Keep believing. Who knows? Maybe this happened because" — Jacque checked off a few inward qualities God was probably fashioning as a result of outward circumstances. Ironclad faith. Robust character. Sensitivity to others. But finally a heavier silence fell. Diana already knew all those things.

She could tie any of us in a tangle of theological thread from her years of Bible study, not to mention a masters degree in counseling. She knew the doctrinal ropes; she had spoon-fed me "suffering develops patience" and "suffering refines faith" when I kept bugging her as to "why?" Diana was doing that thirty years ago.

Slowly, out of the silence, a song began. First faintly, then swelling as all joined in:

> Sometimes I feel discouraged,
>   and think my work's in vain,
> but then the Holy Spirit
>   revives my soul again.

The old favorite from Young Life Club days came rising out of our memories as though we were saddle-shoed teenagers again, sitting cross-legged on the church-hall floor.

> There is a balm in Gilead
>   To make the wounded whole;
> There is a balm in Gilead
>   To heal the sin-sick soul.

It was an old spiritual inspired by the prophet Jeremiah who, amidst the horror of the Babylonian invasion, asked, "Is there no balm in Gilead? Is there no physician there? Why then is there no healing for the wound of my people?" (Jeremiah 8:22). Back in high school, we sang about God, the balm in Gilead, to soothe a wounded heart from a sophomore crush. But now the lyrics glowed with a smooth patina from years tarnished by divorce, paralysis, disease, and drugs.

We sang the last note, then Connie sighed, "Dessert, anyone?"

Mrs. Filbert got up and began clearing the table. Chairs shuffled, dishes clinked, and the room filled with pleasant chatter. As coffee was served, I sat back and realized I had just passed—we all passed through—a new milestone.

When your heart is being wrung out like a sponge, an orderly list of "sixteen good biblical reasons as to why this is happening" can sting like salt in a wound. You don't stop the bleeding that way. A checklist may be okay when you're looking at your suffering in a rearview mirror, but when you're hurting in the present tense, "Let me explain why this is happening" isn't always livable.

Answers, no matter how good they are, cannot be the *coup de grace*. Purified faith is never an end in itself; it culminates in God. Stronger character is character made muscular not for its own sake, but God's. A livelier hope is more spirited because of its focus on the Lord. To forget this is to tarnish faith, weaken character, and deflate hope. "If you have these qualities existing and growing in you then it means that knowing our Lord Jesus Christ has not made your lives either complacent or unproductive" (2 Peter 1:8 Phillips).

We must never distance the Bible's answers from God. I once heard Dr. Peter Kreeft say that the problem of suffering is not about some *thing*, but *Someone*. It follows that the answer must not be something, but Someone. "Knowing our Lord Jesus Christ" is keeping your eye on the Sculptor—not on the suffering or even suffering's benefits.

Besides, answers are for the head. They don't always reach the problem where it hurts—in the gut and the heart. When people are sorely suffering, like my friend Diana, they are like hurting children looking up into the faces of their parents, crying and asking, "Daddy, why?" Those children don't want explanations, answers, or "reasons why"; they want their daddy to pick them up, pat them on the back, and reassure them that everything is going to be okay.

Our heartfelt plea is for assurance—Fatherly assurance—that there is an order to reality that far transcends our problems. We want to know that, somehow, *everything will be okay.*

We amble on along our philosophical path, then—BAM!—we get hit with suffering. No longer is our fundamental view of life providing a sense of meaning or a sense of security in our world. Suffering has not only rocked the boat, it's capsized it. We need assurance that the world is not splitting apart at the seams. We need to know we aren't going to fizzle into a zillion atomic particles and go spinning off in space. We need to be reassured that the world, the universe, is not in nightmarish chaos, but orderly and stable.

God must be at the center of things. He must be in the center of our suffering. What's more, He must be our Daddy. Personal and compassionate. This is our cry.

God, like a father, doesn't just give advice. He gives Himself. He becomes the husband to the grieving widow (Isaiah 54:5). He becomes the comforter to the barren woman (Isaiah 54:1). He becomes the father of the orphaned (Psalm 10:14). He becomes the bridegroom to the single person (Isaiah 62:5). He is the healer to the sick (Exodus 15:26). He is the wonderful counselor to the confused and depressed (Isaiah 9:6).

He is our hope.

He is our shield and very great reward.

This is what you do when someone you love is in anguish; you respond to the pleas of their heart by giving them your heart. If you are the One at the center of the universe holding it together, if everything moves, breathes, and has its being in you, you can do no more than give yourself (Acts 17:28).

It's the only answer that ultimately matters.

It is the only hope that truly satisfies.[6]

Back at the Pool of Bethesda

A flurry of dust swirled at my feet as a warm, dry breeze rose and tossed my hair. I was speechless here. Large tears welled in my eyes, and I sniffed hard, as I imagined blind people clustered against the wall and the lame leaning against the pillars. I could see paralyzed people lying on stretchers and mats, their eyes searching and their hands pleading.

And I saw myself among them—just as I had so many years before—a scruffy, sun-browned young girl dressed in a burlap cloak, lying on a mat, squeezed somewhere between a shady cool wall and the paralyzed man who had been there for thirty-eight years.

Another dry breeze touched my wet face.

Oh Lord, You waited more than thirty years—almost as many years as the paralyzed man You healed that day—to bring me to this place.

I gulped hard, remembering the times I'd lain numb and depressed in my hospital bed, hoping and praying that Jesus would heal me, that He would come to my bedside as He did with the man on the straw mat, that He would see me and not pass me by. I remembered the times Diana would read to me about this place, and the film clip that looped in my mind, playing over and over again.

Ken waved at me from way down in the ruins.

"You won't believe how many times I used to picture myself here," I called, my voice echoing across the crumbled stones and columns. Ken nodded, continuing to explore below.

I couldn't expect him to understand how much I had invested myself in this place years ago and far, far away.

I leaned on my arm against the guardrail.

"And now … after thirty years … I'm here," I whispered. "I made it."

That's when it hit me. Jesus *didn't* pass me by. He didn't overlook me. He didn't walk away. I had never been able to see the end to that movie loop in my imagination, but I could see it now.

Jesus had truly come my way and answered my prayer.

And His answer was no.

I turned my thoughts, my words, heavenward.

Lord, Your no answer to physical healing meant yes to a deeper healing. And a better one. Your answer has bound me to other believers and taught me so much about myself. It's purged sin from my life; it's strengthened my commitment to You. Forced me to depend on Your grace. Your wiser, deeper answer has stretched my hope, refined my faith, and helped me to know You better. And You are good. You are so good.

I let the tears fall.

I know I wouldn't know You … I wouldn't love and trust You … were it not for—

I looked down at my paralyzed legs.

—for this wheelchair. Thank You, Lord, for this chair.

Ken returned to my side, his chest heaving and his hands cupped. "Look," he said excitedly, "I have something for you." He extended his hands. "Water from the Pool of Bethesda. I found it way down at the bottom of some steps. It was pitch black—and scary. But I got some for you."

A brisk wind rumpled our shirts as Ken placed cool, wet hands on my forehead. "Lord," he prayed, "thank You for my wife."

There are more important things in life than walking.

I cried and laughed at the same time. Ken's prayer was like a capstone, a seal on a most remarkable day. We said good-bye to the Pool of Bethesda, and as we walked back up the path toward the Lion's Gate, I glanced back and shook my head in amazement.

It wasn't often I could presuppose God's motives, but I could this one. He had brought me to that Pool, the Pool I had seen over and over in my dreams, that I might make an altar of remembrance out of the ruins. That I might see—and thank Him for—the wiser choice, the better answer, the harder yet richer path.

He had brought me here, all the way from home—halfway around the earth—so I could declare it to anyone within earshot of the whole universe, to anyone who might care.

And that was the ruby of wisdom, so very valuable, so terribly hard-won.

There are more important things in life than walking.

Better by Far

I looked forward to Steve coming all day. Now the evening is over and everything is still. Winter still. Moonlight still. Midnight still.

My friend and I spent another evening sitting by a snapping, popping, cherry-wood fire in the fireplace. It smelled wonderful.

As at other times, Steve brought his Bible. He read some and we talked. When the subject turned to heaven, it really got my attention. Since I was a little girl I've wondered about it. We used to sing,

> *This world is not my home,*
> *I'm just a-passin' through;*
> *my treasures are laid up,*
> *somewhere beyond the blue.*

I've never really had any trouble believing in a heaven, but it all seemed so vague to me. *Somewhere beyond the blue.* Everyone wants to go there, but where is it? What does it look like? Who is there, what do they wear, and what do they do?

Steve began to read to me from 1 Corinthians 15 — the part

about the new bodies we will have after we leave this world. Again, he had my full attention. He called that future body a "glorified body," and he began to think out loud about all the amazing things an immortal body could do. Run without ever getting tired. Enjoy endless daylight without needing sleep. Move through walls and from place to place, as Jesus did after He rose from the dead. And who knows? Maybe even fly.

To me, the best thought was that I would no longer be paralyzed. If I had just that much and no more, it would be enough. To walk away from my wheelchair forever. To never again have to depend on others for everything I need and everything I do. I couldn't help imagining along with him—thinking about all the things I would be able to do with new hands, new arms, and new legs. Flying? Who cares. Walking through walls. Who needs to? Running for a thousand years and never stopping to catch your breath? Fine. But what's the point?

I would be happy just to walk a few steps to the window, pull back the curtain, and look out at the falling snow. Or brush my hair. Or peel an orange. And then ... later ... maybe I could sprint across an open field, scale a few rocks, or skip through a meadow.

For a few minutes, as Steve kept reading to me in that gentle, earnest voice of his, I got caught up in something like a vision. My heart filled with longing. Just for a moment—even though I was stuck in my wheelchair and unable to move—I remembered what it felt like to be really free.

Steve could see what was happening to me, bless his heart, and kept reading more passages. As he turned to one more description in the book of Revelation, I couldn't wait to read all about this future God was reserving for us.

But that's when it all began to unravel for me.

Steve read:

> Then I saw a new heaven and a new earth.... (Revelation 21:1)

Yes, I could buy that. Everyone knows this old planet of ours is in need of repair.

> ... For the first heaven and the first earth had passed away.... (Revelation 21:2)

That stopped me. The whole earth is going to pass away? There are lots of things I like about earth. Chili dogs with cheese. The NBA playoffs. Bridal Veil Falls at Yosemite National Park. Horses galloping through a wide green field. Starry summer nights. And it's all going away? To be replaced by what?

> And there was no longer any sea....

No sea? No ocean? No smell of salt in the air? No splashing in the breakers? No digging toes into the warm sand?

> I saw the Holy City, the new Jerusalem, coming down out of heaven from God, prepared as a bride beautifully dressed for her husband.

No ocean beaches? No sunrise over Chesapeake Bay? No sand dunes? No Great Barrier Reef? No wheat fields or sequoia trees or daffodils? And really, who cares about some new big city coming out of the sky! I hate cities—even if they are holy. Who wants some monster housing project in the center of heaven? Some people might get excited about a continent-sized gated community with walls two hundred feet thick, but not me.

Steve sensed my disappointment and looked up from his Bible, puzzled. That moment of feeling free and excited about the future vanished like a puff of smoke up the chimney. The plain truth is, I'm stuck in a wheelchair, paralyzed, for the rest of this life on earth, however long that may be. And after that? Well, maybe heaven won't be so great, either.

The more he read, the more it turned me off. It was like some bad description from a Triple-A tour book. Pearl-studded gates. Gold

asphalt. No need to eat, so I guess that means no food. No roast tur-
key. No mashed potatoes and gravy. No pecan pie. No fresh-brewed
coffee. No need to sleep, so there are no beds — or crisp sheets or
downy pillows or hand-stitched quilts. No sunsets, no full moons,
no summer twilights, no starry nights. And oh, by the way: no marriage, either, so no sex.

Hey, but don't miss the architectural wonder that is the New Jerusalem, that striking city of the future. Twelve foundations. Twelve
gates, each gate made of a single pearl.

Welcome to ruby slippers and Somewhere-Over-the-Rainbow.

Heaven is Oz.

Somehow, all the light and joy seemed to be pulled right out of
the living room. The fire still danced on the hearth, but I felt cold.
I couldn't help feeling sorry for Steve, because I couldn't seem to
stop the spiral.

He tried to change the tone. He flipped to Jesus' words in John
14 (verses 1–4).

> Do not let your hearts be troubled. Trust in God; trust also
> in me. In my Father's house are many rooms; if it were not so, I
> would have told you. I am going there to prepare a place for you.
> And if I go and prepare a place for you, I will come back and
> take you to be with me that you also may be where I am. You
> know the way to the place where I am going.

I know what he was trying to do. He was trying to excite my
imagination again. Trying to recapture the wonder I had felt. But it
was like trying to catch a sun ray in a Mason jar.

"Just think of it Joni," he said. "If Jesus is presently preparing
heaven, it must be out-of-sight. It only took Him seven days to create the earth and the whole universe, and hey, He's had almost *two
thousand years* to work on our rooms in His Father's house!"

It was a clever maneuver, but it dive-bombed. You can get bored in the most beautiful hotel room in just a few days. What would it be like to be bored for eternity?

To give him credit, he backed up and took another run at it. He tried explaining that all this stuff about mansions and rooms was probably allegorical anyway. And that was supposed to comfort me somehow? After a few more tries, he smiled a sad smile at me, closed his Bible, fished for something encouraging to say, and finally said good-night.

Now it's late at night, and I'm lying in my bed looking at the pale light from a full moon flooding through my bedroom window. I want to throw back the covers, get out of bed, and look, but there's no way. I can't. But I know the moon must be shining on the wintry fields outside, tracing the maple branches in silver, casting faint shadows on the snow.

Moonlight on a paralyzed girl's bed. Well, that's something. Something I can at least see. Thoughts of heaven had teased my heart and danced just out of reach for a moment or two, but now it all seems a million miles away.

FORTY YEARS LATER
AGOURA HILLS, CALIFORNIA

It doesn't now.

Heaven doesn't seem far away at all. I'm countless miles and forty-one years closer. It may be over the next hill or around the next bend in the road or maybe a little farther than that.

But it's close.

Sometimes I think I can see the glow — like when you're driving out in the desert late at night, and see the lights of a city miles over the horizon.

Heaven will not only be more than we can imagine, the "more" will go on forever. It will be timeless.

It *has* to be.

Joy flows from God, God is eternal; therefore, so is joy. You instinctively know this when you are gripped by a timeless moment, an experience so precious, so perfect, you wish it could last forever.

One early summer morning my sister Jay and I drove down to the little Maryland farming community of Sykesville to visit Grandma Clark. She wasn't really my grandmother. She and Jay had become friends at their tiny stone church on top of the hill, and we had been invited to her big farmhouse for tea. I wheeled into the kitchen and was greeted by the aroma of a hot cake from the oven. Grandma had placed white crisp linen on a table by an open window. A breeze lifted lace curtains and wafted in the scent of hydrangeas.

Jay and I sipped tea from delicate cups. My eyes followed Grandma Clark. She leaned back, smoothed the tablecloth with her hand, and spoke of heaven in grand and wistful terms.

A gust of wind suddenly whipped the curtains, tossing her gray hair. She held up her hand, smiling and squinting against the stiff breeze. *Whooosh!* It eddied around the table, dizzying and lifting our spirits.

The moment was delightfully strange.

I don't know how else to say it, but I think all of us knew that something unusual — and wonderful — had just occurred. It was something more sensed than spoken.

But as quickly as it came, it vanished, settling us back down and becoming timeless, leaving in its wake peace and joy. I can still taste the cakes and tea, inhale the fragrance of spring flowers, see the curtains snap, and dapples of sun dance on the tablecloth.

Moments like these remind us of some other time or place. We say the same of childhood memories: lazy, late afternoons, licking Popsicles on the back step, listening to a lawnmower up the street, and feeling a breeze cool our brow. Or running out the screen door after dinner to catch fireflies. Or by a campfire, hugging our knees, watching the sparks fly upward, becoming stars. If we could be transported back, we'd discover that even as children we felt the same nostalgia, the "remembering" of places and times where we have never been.

It's an indefinable longing, soul-deep. It's a yearning, as C. S. Lewis put it, to pass through the beauty and reach the other side. And in those timeless moments, we hear a whisper without words … but the meaning is something like this: *One day you will bathe in peace like this … satisfaction will shower you … this joy will last forever.*

This is what we as children feel. It's another hint of heaven, like choosing the happiest point in your life and having time stand still.

I'll admit, I've been thinking more and more these days about the life waiting for me on the Other Side. About going home. About departing to be with my Lord.

That tiny flicker of a vision I experienced so many years ago as I sat by the fireside with Steve Estes is now full-bloom. *I want to go*—as much as I've wanted to go anywhere in all of my life, in all of my memory.

I know what you're thinking. What's up with Joni? Maybe it sounds morbid to you. Like a death wish. I don't mean that at all. My health is good enough; I love my husband, my colleagues, my friends, my home, ten thousand lovely places on this earth; and I'm more passionate than ever about the work God has given me to do across the world. There's no funk, no depression. Physical paralysis hasn't paralyzed my spirit for many years.

But there is this …

I've lived with quadriplegia for decades, and being in a wheelchair that long, well, sometimes I wonder. I wonder how much more time I have on earth before I get the call from the Lord to come home.

The call.

Will it be a simple word … *"Joni, come,"* or will it be a shout? Will it be serious, like a whisper in a cathedral, or full of merriment and joy? Will it be a journey, or will an angel simply take me by the hand and draw me through an open window into the sweet morning air of heaven?

Just thinking these thoughts stirs a longing in the deepest places of my spirit, and truly, I am comforted by that anticipation.

When I was still a teenager, trying to come to terms with the thought of a lifetime in a wheelchair, there were times when the thought of heaven wasn't much comfort at all. I would take the specific descriptions that I saw in the Scriptures—which are really all we have—and try to picture myself there. I so much wanted it to be a place like all the dearest and most well-loved places I have known on earth.

> I wanted to put on jeans and a flannel shirt, walk on crunchy fall leaves, and smell wet fields and wood smoke on the cool autumn breeze.
>
> I wanted to ride a horse along a snow-covered country lane.
>
> I wanted to pick wild roses along the wooden fence in the back pasture.
>
> I wanted to see the Milky Way on a crisp December night, far away from the glare of city lights.

Heaven? It all seemed so distant and ethereal, the images wispy and thin. Something between a Sunday school paper sketch and a half-remembered dream. I needed a vision of the next life desperately because the thought of an earthly life of paralysis stretching out before me for years and years was almost more than my soul could bear.

I *needed* to be excited about heaven, just to keep my sanity, just to give my mind somewhere to go to escape the prison of my broken body. But who could get worked up over some misty Twilight Zone where birds incessantly chirp, angels bounce from cloud to cloud, and eternal organ music (heavy with tremolo) fills every corner of paradise?

We are victimized by what people have said, spoken, illustrated, or sang about the Coming Age. We've seen the magazine cartoons with Saint Peter sitting at a desk in the clouds, guarding a gate. We've heard the nineteenth-century gospel songs that make us think of starchy dark suits, shined shoes, proper Sunday dresses, stern faces, and long (eternal) sermons. We've seen classic art depictions, with halos, pale, womanly angels, and God with a long white beard.

We've been filled up to our eyebrows with clichés, parodies, kitsch, and tedious two-dimensional paintings of a place we'd never even want to visit, let alone live in forever.

I wanted something more. I wanted a place to dream of, hold onto, think about in those long hours of enforced stillness on my bed. To me, it didn't seem like I was asking for a lot. Maybe just a few snapshots from the other side — grainy, black and white, out of focus, it didn't matter. Anything that would give me the most basic mental image of a reality so far beyond my reach.

But Scripture gave me images I simply couldn't process. Harps. Crowns. Rainbow thrones. Big rambling mansions. Fantastic angelic beings with multiple faces, eyes tucked under wings, and wheels within wheels, resounding like thunder. A sea of glass. A river flowing through a temple. An altar with martyred saints underneath. A city the size of Australia dropping out of the sky.

None of it touched my heart.

I think back to those days — so many years ago now — and wish I could bring a new perspective to that young girl in her strange new wheelchair, trying so hard to find her way in an alien, frightening world where everything had changed. Strange as it may sound, I've wanted to somehow travel back in time and sit beside her — wheelchair alongside wheelchair — and speak to her, heartbroken and lost as she was.

What would I say? How could I comfort her?

"Joni ... you want heaven to be real, and it is. You want it to be a Place, a Destination, home that will remind you of everything you have loved best in this life, and it will be.

"But here is the truth ... a ruby, hard-won ... the real truth sifted and refined through countless tears, untold hours of prayer, and many years of paralysis. It isn't thinking about a Place that will lift your heart and make your sorrow easier to bear. It's a Person. It's Jesus.

> *It isn't thinking about a Place that will lift your heart and make your sorrow easier to bear. It's a Person. It's Jesus. ... Heaven will be heaven because He is there.*

"Heaven isn't heaven because of what you will see or what you will do or where you will go. Halos and gold freeways? Set all that aside for now. Heaven will be heaven because He is there. Physically. Visibly. Gloriously. Eternally.

"I know ... you need to escape sometimes. To slip away in your thoughts to something other than a routine that seems hurtful and hateful to you. The images of heaven you encounter in the Bible trouble you because you can't wrap your mind around them. The language is cryptic. You almost have to crack heaven's hieroglyphics before any of it makes sense. You're looking for a place where your spirit can rest, but you get lost in the bowls, scrolls, and trumpets of Revelation.

"That's okay, for now. Someday it will all make sense. For now, just set your thoughts on Jesus. You can't wrap your mind around Him, either, but He will wrap His arms around you. The more you learn of Him, think of Him, fill your eyes with Him, the more you will find the comfort you crave in your brokenness. He is so impossibly far beyond anything you have ever imagined or conceived Him to be.

"Don't think of cheesy color plates from children's Bibles, vacation-Bible-school curriculum, medieval paintings, or stained-glass windows. That would be like mistaking your best friend for a crayon image from a four-year-old. This is the One who created music and starlight, cherries and summer roses, a man's strong touch and a woman's laughter, snow-capped mountains and April rain, a baby's eyelashes and vast planets where no one has walked but angels.

"Consider Him.

"Adore Him."

I See Heaven Open ...

If we're trying to draw comfort from imagined scenes of heaven—celestial mountains and fields, valleys and vistas—our comfort will be as thin as the limits of our imagination.

That's because the eyes of our heart are looking in the wrong place. Visions of heavenly cities, no matter how radiant, how stunning will never sustain us in an hour of deep trial. It has to be more. Much more.

It must be a person.

In the book of Acts, before the first stones began to strike the back and arms and face of Stephen, God sent a vision to sustain him in those terrible moments.

The veil between time and eternity was swept aside, like a curtain pushed away from an open window by the wind, and Stephen's earthly eyes were enabled to see into heaven. How many scenes and vistas from how many corners of heaven might the Holy Spirit have chosen to show this man on the edge of martyrdom? Towering waterfalls? Endless fields of green? Galaxy wide nebula with colors beyond the spectrum?

God could have picked anything.

Instead, He picked the one thing that would fill His servant's heart with joy beyond anything else—even in the shock and pain of a stoning.

> But Stephen, full of the Holy Spirit, looked up to heaven and saw the glory of God, and Jesus standing at the right hand

of God. "Look," he said, "I see heaven open and the Son of Man standing at the right hand of God." (Acts 7:55–56)

The last thing Stephen saw on this earth wasn't on earth at all. It was the Lord Jesus, standing, arms open wide, ready to sweep this first martyr into His embrace. And do you think He had a smile of welcome on His face? I can't imagine anything else.

If you need a bit more convincing that heaven is more about a Person than a place, then take this test St. Augustine gave his students centuries ago. Imagine Jesus appeared to you and said, "You want heaven? I'll make a deal with you. I'll give you anything and everything you ask. Nothing will be sin. Nothing will be forbidden, and everything will be possible for you. You will never be bored and you will never die. Only ... you will never see My face."

Brrr! Do you feel that chill in your soul? Your heart and mind recoil in unison. As a son or daughter of God, your deepest desire — beyond anything else in the world — is to see your Redeemer. Like St. Augustine said of God, "Thou has made us for Thyself, and therefore our hearts are restless until they rest in Thee."[7]

Yes, your heart's home is in the heart of God. He has placed within you a yearning for Himself, a desire to know and understand what He is like. Every soul feels the void and the emptiness until it connects with its Maker.

> Like tides on a crescent sea-beach,
>   When the moon is new and thin,
> Into our hearts high yearnings
>   Come welling and surging in.
> Come from the mystic ocean,
>   Whose rim no foot has trod,
> Some of us call it longing,
>   And others call it God.[8]

Pleasures and treasures on earth may be sought after and not found, but only God comes with the guarantee that He *will* be found. "You will seek me and find me when you seek me with all your heart. I will be found by you" (Jeremiah 29:13–14).

More specifically, He will be found in Jesus Christ. God illumines our heart and mind when we sincerely search for the Truth and reveals Jesus, the photo image of the Father who dwells in unapproachable light. Jesus is the source of every longing we've ever had about heaven. Jesus is God wearing a human face. He is real and not abstract. He invites us to do what we cannot do with the incomprehensible—He invites us to drink and eat of Him, and "taste and see that the LORD is good" (Psalm 34:8).

Jesus is sunshine to our heart. Not just to our logic, but our heart. Praise God, we know the answer to our heart's longing. It's Jesus!

The disciples of Jesus, at first, weren't so sure that this Man in their midst would fulfill their deepest longings, so "Philip said, 'Lord, show us the Father and that will be enough for us.' Jesus answered: 'Don't you know me, Philip, even after I have been among you such a long time? Anyone who has seen me has seen the Father'" (John 14:8–9).

Our longings are satisfied in Him for "the Son is the radiance of God's glory and the exact representation of his being" (Hebrews 1:3). We can know God—our Father in heaven—if we know Jesus. And knowing Him, as we would desire to know a Lover, is ecstasy. His invitation to "enter into the joy of the Lord" (Matthew 25:23 paraphrased) is like stepping into a raft and being carried helplessly along a surging current, spilling over and splashing with joy.

I'll bet Charles Wesley was enraptured when he penned the fourth stanza to his hymn "Love Divine, All Loves Excelling":

> *Finish then Thy new creation,*
> *Pure and spotless let us be;*
> *Let us see Thy great salvation*
> *Perfectly restored in Thee:*
> *Changed from glory into glory,*
> *Till in heav'n we take our place,*
> *Till we cast our crowns before Thee,*
> *Lost in wonder, love and praise!*

Tears have streamed down my cheeks in church when I've sung that last line. Heaven is a place, and also a Person in whom I am lost in wonder, love, and praise.

Better by Far ...

In the book of Philippians, Paul was in a Roman prison for his faith in Christ, facing the very real prospect of a quick execution. Not knowing how long he had to live, he wrote these words to the church at Philippi ... and to us.

> For to me, to live is Christ and to die is gain. If I am to go on living in the body, this will mean fruitful labor for me. Yet what shall I choose? I do not know! I am torn between the two: I desire to depart and be with Christ, which is better by far. (Philippians 1:21–23)

In the King James Version, Paul says, "I am in a strait betwixt two." It was a seesaw tug of war in his soul. Paul was being pulled first toward heaven then toward earth, back and forth.

I am torn.... I desire to depart and be with Christ....

The Greek word translated "desire" speaks of a strong passion or urge, a growing or swelling emotion. It's an excitement. A passion. A thought that sweeps you along and almost consumes you.

The word translated "depart" pictures a ship that has been loosed from its moorings, finally free to do what it was destined and designed to do.

Sail.

Yes, he was ready and more than ready to cut loose his anchor and set sail for the destination that waited just beyond his vision and made him homesick for a land he'd never seen. But the apostle wasn't thinking about a location as much as he was thinking about the best Friend he had ever known in all his years. He wanted to be *with* Christ. In one sense, the celestial coordinates didn't really matter. Wherever Jesus was, that would be heaven.

He wanted to depart. He was ready and more than ready to exchange one life for another. Being with Christ, he said, would be *better* by far. It was no contest. If the door opened, he would *leap* at the opportunity.

That prospect sustained him. How else could he have lived those years in Roman captivity, whether through house arrest or in the fetid depths of a dungeon? How else could he have written one of the greatest treatises on joy ever penned with iron shackles on his wrists and ankles, and a body so bruised, broken, and scarred from savage beatings?

It wasn't because he needed a "get away" and fantasized about another place. He wasn't saying, "Well, there's a pretty beach on Cyprus that I like, and there's heaven too." He wasn't saying, "I can't wait to run my hand up and down that smooth gate of pearl and see those heavenly trees bearing fruit by that crystal river." No, it wasn't a location that drew him, delighted him, and consumed him. It was the prospect of finding himself wholly in the presence of the One who was life itself to him.

Once in the middle of the day in the middle of a journey in the middle of his life, he had been swept off his mount by a supernova, searing his eyes, blasting the breath from his lungs, and flooding every crease and crevice in his soul. And he would spend the rest of his days seeking, serving, and worshiping the One whose very name is Light.

Earlier in his letter, he wrote, "I am ready for anything through the strength of the one who lives within me" (Philippians 4:13 Phillips). He wasn't drawing strength from some snapshot of heavenly Real Estate, some slick, color brochure of the New Jerusalem — even though he probably had such vivid mental images from his previous visit to "the third heaven."

It wasn't any place. It wasn't any GPS location in the physical universe or the heavenlies.

It was Jesus.

It was the Bright, Morning Star. It was the Son of God. It was the Savior, once humbled, but now in His rightful place in the highest heaven. It was the Weaver of Light, the Source of Beauty, the Wellspring of Music, the Artesian Fountain of truth and joy and justice and peace and laughter and hope and kindness and everything worth having in this old world of ours or the next.

Oh, to be there when my Jesus—yes, He's mine—steps on to the center stage of the universe to be crowned as King of kings and Lord of lords. It will be His day, His moment, and best of all, His opportunity to turn up the wattage on the Father's glory. For if anyone, anywhere in the universe still harbors doubt that God was unjust—that He dirtied His hands—by saving sinners like me, Jesus will finally put those doubts to rest. He will show that God didn't circumvent justice by redeeming people; rather, God wrapped justice in mercy when He sent His precious, perfect Son to die in our place.

It's all about *Jesus.*

And I want to be there when the universe falls back on its heels in utter amazement over what Jesus has done! For if it weren't for Jesus—if He had not gone to the cross—no one would ever see the mercy of God; if it weren't for Jesus, no one could ever grasp the compassion of God; if it weren't for Jesus, I dare say God's most glorious attributes might remain hidden for all of eternity. Oh, I want to be there among the cheering throngs, when we praise and bless God for His *mercy* and *grace!*

The apostle Paul wasn't living in denial as he languished in those rusty chains; he simply adjusted his longings in light of the sufficiency of Christ. Jesus was more than enough whether Paul was "well fed or hungry, whether living in plenty or in want" (Philippians 4:12).

In those early years of my injury, I had been longing for Another Place. A beautiful, unspoiled land where I could go in my mind when the weight of life felt like it was going to crush me. I looked through the Bible for that place, but no description drew me. No biblical sketch drew my heart. I knew that "this world is not my home," but the next world didn't seem all that appealing to me, either.

Our hope, once again, is not a what, but a Who. The hope we wait for, our only hope, is the "blessed hope—the glorious appearing of our great God and Savior, Jesus Christ" (Titus 2:13). It is Jesus we've travailed all this suffering for—not a slice of celestial Real Estate. Our hope is for the Desire of the Nations, the Healer of Broken Hearts, the Friend of Sinners. True, we are waiting for a party. But more accurately, we are waiting for the Person who will make it a party.

Heaven will be glorious beyond any description because I will be at His side, walk and talk with Him.

Here is the ruby, hard-won. It wasn't a vision of a Place that would comfort me. It was the presence of a real Person. Earth is tolerable because of what I can see of Jesus. And heaven will be glorious beyond any description because I will be at His side, walk and talk with Him. And worship at last as I was always meant to worship, but never could.

A Failing Tent

The apostle Paul was a missionary by calling but a tentmaker by trade. During his ministry in Corinth, he stayed with a fellow tentmaker named Aquila. So the two men would ply their craftsmanship in the tent shop during the week, and then Paul would go into the synagogue on Sabbath days and reason with the Jews and Greeks.

Years later, when he was writing to the church at Corinth, he must have been reminded of those days with Aquila, because he wove some tent imagery into his letter. Speaking of the contrast between this earthly life and the life in heaven to come, he wrote:

> Now we know that if the earthly tent we live in is destroyed, we have a building from God, an eternal house in heaven, not built by human hands. Meanwhile we groan, longing to be clothed with our heavenly dwelling, because when we are clothed, we will not be found naked. For while we are in this tent, we groan and are burdened, because we do not wish to be unclothed but to be clothed with our heavenly dwelling, so that what is mortal may be swallowed up by life. (2 Corinthians 5:1–4)

When we went beach camping as kids, I thought living in a tent was the ultimate adventure.

Sand on the canvas floor? Who cares! Mosquitoes? Just get out the mosquito netting. Rain? Break out the tarps and pull down the canvas flaps. Dirt? Hey, a little dirt never hurt anyone. Living in a tent (we thought then) was great fun!

Now, many years later, it's a different story. Ken and I have enjoyed a few camping experiences in our married life, but I can only take it for so long. For some reason, tent camping gets a little more strenuous with each passing year. Sand, mosquitoes, dirt, rain? *You can have it*, I say to myself after four or five days.

Maybe that's why Paul the tentmaker likened living in these bodies of ours to occupying a tent. Unless you happen to be a Bedouin out in the Arabian desert, a tent is only meant to be temporary housing. We can only take it for so long. And with each passing year, we find living in these bodies of ours more strenuous than the year before.

Paul says, "We groan."

And the older we get, the more we do it. Aren't you glad we won't always be "groaning and burdened" with these patchwork tents of ours?

When I think along these lines, I'm reminded of Steve Coyle.

Steve, who lived in Hawaii, went swimming for an hour each morning. One day a diving accident badly bruised his spinal column. He recovered from that mishap, but just three months later had another accident which left him a quadriplegic. Even so, Steve never complained about his disability. He always managed to work in some words of praise to the Lord in all his conversation.

I wish the story got better from there, but the truth is, Steve then developed cancer. He suffered greatly and, after losing over eighty pounds, went to be with the Lord. How he must have grown weary of his tent!

Shortly before he died, Steve wanted to record some of his thoughts in verse. He entrusted the lines to a nurse friend. Here are the last two stanzas, as he reflects on a tent that was falling apart and near collapse.

> *I went to Him on bended knees*
> *Begging Him, "Oh Tentmaker please!*
> *Restore this tent I thought would last,*
> *This canvas house that went so fast."*
>
> *He looked at me through loving eyes*
> *And merely pointed to the skies.*
> *"Please don't grieve over some old tent,*
> *Old canvas walls that have been spent*
> *For this mansion that's been built by Me*
> *Will last you for eternity."*

With that assurance, Steve gladly broke camp and moved on.

My tent too is giving way. The pegs are loose in the ground, the cords are frayed, and the tent frame has bent, giving way to long years and rough weather.

Back in the old days, canvas tents were supported by interior wooden tent poles. If you drove somewhere in the wilderness to go camping and then realized you'd left the tent poles at home, you were in for a difficult experience. It's hard to sleep, eat, and read by lantern light — or do most anything — in a collapsed tent.

Paralysis is something like that. Many survive with it, and life goes on. But it makes everything so difficult. And after awhile, you want to say, "Enough already, let's just go home!"

As Paul continued his tent metaphor to the church in Corinth, he went on to say: "Therefore we are always confident and know that as long as we are at home in the body [this earthly tent] we are away from the Lord. We live by faith, not by sight. We ... would prefer to be away from the body and at home with the Lord" (2 Corinthians 5:6, 7).

In other words, I'll live with this old tent, as difficult and painful as it may be, and sustain myself with faith in God. But what would I *rather* do? I'd rather break camp and go home to Jesus.

Let's Go Home

Antonin Dvořák's *New World Symphony* has been one the most well-loved and often-performed symphonies for years.

If you're familiar at all with this music, you could quickly identify a repeating musical theme that weaves its way in and out of the Largo movement of Dvořák's creation. Whenever I hear it, it stirs a longing in my heart. Is it the haunting melody that does it, or is it because the theme was lifted from an old Negro spiritual with heart-tugging lyrics?

> *Goin' home, goin' home, I'm a-goin' home;*
> *Quiet-like, some still day, I'm jes' a-goin' home.*
>> *It's not far, jes' close by,*
>>> *Through an open door;*
>> *Work all done, care laid by,*
>>> *Gwine to fear no more.*
>
> *Mother's there 'spectin' me,*
>> *Father's waitin' too;*

Lots o' folk gather'd there,
All the friends I knew,
All the friends I knew.
Home, I'm goin' home!

But there is more to the story than that. Dvořák, who left his beloved Bohemia (now in the Czech Republic) in 1892, spent three years in New York City, directing the National Conservatory of Music. And in those years, in the crowded, bustling streets and sidewalks of the big city, he became desperately homesick for his native land. And when those emotions combined with the "homesick-for-heaven" melody of the old spiritual, it became an element of that great work that just seems to embody a longing for home.[9]

Goin' home.

On some days, I feel as though I might be called Home at any moment.

When I get caught up in that "let's go home" emotion, it blends in my memory with long-ago days when I used to play in the woods beyond our backyard. As soon as I got home from elementary school, and while Mom was preparing dinner, I would put my things in my room and race out the back door to play with Kathy and a few neighborhood kids. We would call to each other and our shouts would echo through the tall oak trees. Everything echoed — the chatter of birds, the distant clatter of an old lawnmower, the slamming of screen doors. Our play was so much fun that an hour would go by and I'd hardly realize it. I barely noticed the rays of the sinking sun cutting long shadows through the trees.

Kathy and I knew that soon Mother would call us home.

Funny, I rarely took it upon myself to go home unless called. Something in me wanted to hear that call ... the sound of Daddy's or Mom's voice through cupped hands, shouting my name. No sooner did I hope they'd call when I would hear the familiar ding-ding-a-ling-ding of the dinner bell by the back door.

"Supper's ready ... time to come home!"

It's odd how I can still hear Mother's voice. It almost makes me cry; it just about made me cry when I was a child. The echo of the bell ... the haunting sound through the woods ... the joy about to break open my heart for the love of home, the warmth of family ... not to mention fried chicken and mashed potatoes by a glowing fire in the living room. And often during the summer after the table was cleared and dessert was over, we'd sit in the backyard and watch the sun go down.

"There it goes ..."

"It's almost gone ... just a little tip of light left."

Our family would vie for who'd be the last one to see the sun set.

And then we'd wait for the stars to come out, singing hymns and counting the constellations. It was all I could hope for as a kid. And here I am an adult still looking beyond Ursa Major, singing heaven's melodies, and winning victories until earth's twilight gives way to the dawn of eternity.

And in that dawn, be it red-gold, pale blue and purple, or pearl gray, dissolving into colors beyond the spectrum, I will catch my first glimpse of the place I have dreamed of ten thousand times since I gazed into the endless depths of a summer sky as a little girl. It will be new, but it won't be strange to me. It will be the back roads of Maryland, the early morning shimmer on Chesapeake Bay, the crash of surf on a warm California beach, and the patches of impossible blue between the pine trees in the high Sierras. It will be everything dear and familiar scrubbed clean, rain-washed with joy, and multiplied a million times over.

But more than any celestial landscape, I long for something else even more. His voice, as He stands on the back porch of heaven, calling me home to supper. And when I first catch sight of Him, arms open to welcome me ...

Just watch me run.

9

Why Would He Say No?

It has been three weeks now, and nothing has changed. My body still hasn't got the message.

I give the mental command to my fingers and toes. *Move!* And there's nothing. Nothing at all. Okay, so it will be a gradual change. I can handle that. I'll wake up in the morning and feel the tiniest tingle, a feather-brush across my little finger. Or I'll make a small, small movement of one of my toes—maybe just a thirty-second of an inch. Just a fraction of an inch would be the best thing in the whole world! It would mean a beginning ... a baby's step ... an ant's step ... toward healing.

But for right now, it's the hard work of believing that it's already done. *I'm trying so hard to believe.* Trying so hard to hang onto faith with everything in me. But what if it's not enough? What if I'm not believing hard enough? What if I've allowed the shadow of a doubt? Will that nullify everything?

I had such hopes! (There I go, talking in the past tense, as if healing won't happen. Maybe I've lost faith already.)

A group of us went to an old, picturesque country church with a steeple, not far from home. Friends, family, church leaders, elders, pastors. I had asked them all to come to pray for my healing, and they did. Almost everyone.

We began by reading Scripture out loud—some reading from the New Testament, some reading from the Old. God honors His own Word, right? That's what I've always heard.

Then, as the summer rain beat down on the church roof, some read specific promises from the Bible about healing. And they seem so clear!

> Is any one of you sick? He should call the elders of the church to pray over him and anoint him with oil in the name of the Lord. And the prayer offered in faith will make the sick person well; the Lord will raise him up.

That's right out of the book of James (5:14–15). Others read the stories of those who were healed—like the paralytic man in the book of Mark. Jesus said, "I tell you, get up, take your mat and go home" (2:11). And he did! Just like that.

After we read, they anointed my head with olive oil. Then how we prayed! Hands of many on my head, my shoulders. Such fervent prayer, with tears. Such faith in that room. We asked God to glorify Himself by allowing me to walk again. And I'm telling you, we believed it would happen.

> *So why can't I move? Why am I still in this wheelchair? Oh Lord, didn't You hear us? Did I do it all wrong? Don't You care? I do believe—help my unbelief!*

I didn't get right up out of the wheelchair. But that was okay. The Bible says of the ten lepers, "As *they went*, they were cleansed" (Luke 17:14). So it didn't have to be right then.

Leaving the little church with my prayer team, I felt humbled by it all. How wonderful that God had seen me in my distress and heard the cry of my heart. Exiting through the front door, it was as if heaven was giving us a glorious amen. The rain had stopped, the parking lot was flooded with golden light, the puddles molten gold, and a majestic rainbow burned across the sky in the misty distance.

As the car drove away, I kept saying, "Thank You, Lord! Thank You, Lord," over and over. I knew it had already begun. The feeling would return. The strength would come. I would soar on wings of eagles. I would run and not grow weary, walk and not faint.

Even though nothing had happened (yet), I kept that secret little glow of joy and gratitude alive in my heart all through the evening. I woke up the next morning with strong expectation. This would be the day! Or then again ... maybe tomorrow.

But now the days have come and gone. It's been two weeks, and there's nothing.

I keep fighting off this thought that tries to take over my emotions. *There must be something wrong with me. There must be sin in my life. I must not be believing hard enough.*

But I *know* I had faith. I even called some of my friends the week before the healing service and said, "Watch for me standing on your doorstep soon. I'm going to be healed!"

Still ... it has to be me. It has to be something wrong with me.

FORTY YEARS LATER

I remember those days so well.

~~To be healed of suffering is to be happy.~~

This line of thinking is the path I took in those early weeks and months of dealing with my paralysis.

I tried to imagine what He was thinking. If God were God—I was convinced He was all powerful and loving—He had to be as anxious to relieve my pain as I was. A heavenly Father had to weep over me as my daddy often did, standing by my bedside, white-knuckling the guardrail. I was one of God's children, and God would never do anything to harm one of His own. *Would He?*

Didn't Jesus say, "Which of you fathers, if your son asks for a fish, will give him a snake instead? Or if he asks for an egg, will give him a scorpion? If you then ... know how to give good gifts to your children, how much more will your Father in heaven?" (Luke 11:11–13)?

So I was asking Him for a fish. I was asking Him for an egg. I was begging Him for something good. Wouldn't leaving me in paralysis for the rest of my life be like handing me a loathsome, lethal snake or scorpion? Would a loving Father treat His daughter like that? Of course not! He had to want me healed and whole again.

After a couple of years, I remember thinking to myself, *Maybe I've learned the lesson God wanted to teach me. I'm doing okay in this wheelchair. The suicidal thoughts are gone. Depression comes less frequently. My whole family is a lot closer to the Lord. I'm a bit more patient, and hey, I think I'm doing pretty well without the use of my hands. And didn't the Lord say, "Ask and it will be given to you?" (Matthew 7:7)?*

But how should I ask for healing? I thought of my horse when I was a young girl, of how I had to learn to catch her to put the halter on. No horse wants to be caught. If they see you coming, they gallop away. So when I got within a few yards, I turned and sat with my back to her. Sure enough, within minutes I felt her muzzle on my back. I slowly turned, stroked her forehead, and gently slipped the halter over her head.

Maybe God is that way—maybe He's waiting for me to turn my back on my wish for a healthy body. Or to turn my back on wanting to catch Him. I began to wonder if I should just release my angst, just let it go. Maybe that way, He would come up behind me and give me my wish.

My sister Jay and I heard that Kathryn Kuhlman, a famous faith healer, was coming to the Washington, D.C., Hilton ballroom. Stories had reached us about cancer-ridden people who'd been cured in Philadelphia at one of her crusades. I wondered if I should go to the healing service in Washington, D.C.

One morning, when Jay was putting my legs through my range-of-motion exercises, Ernest Angley came on television. He was an odd sort of man who wore a bad toupee and ill-fitting suits, and Jay and I enjoyed his antics. My sister and I stopped and watched as people dropped their crutches or got up out of their wheelchairs, many raising their hands and declaring they were free from pain.

"Do you think God could heal you?" Jay asked, staring at the screen.

"Maybe it *is* time," I replied. And so, wondering if this might be an answer to the prayers of many, we found our way to Washington Hilton and the packed-out healing service.

I remember the night so well. Miss Kuhlman breezed onto the stage in her white gown, and my heart raced as I prayed, "Lord, the Bible says You heal all our diseases. I'm ready for You to get me out of this wheelchair. Please, would You?"

God answered. And again, His answer was no.

Wheeling away from the crusade that night, I was number fifteen in a line of thirty wheelchair-users waiting to exit at the stadium elevator, all of us trying to make a fast escape ahead of the people on crutches. I remember glancing around at all the disappointed and confused people and thinking, *Something's wrong with this picture. Is this the only way to deal with suffering? Trying desperately to remove it?*

When I looked in the mirror after I got home, I saw their sullen expression staring back. I was just as perplexed as the people near the elevator.

Okay, let me get this straight: God is good. God is love. He is all powerful. Plus, when He walked on earth, He bent over backward to relieve the sufferings of people, everyone from the hemorrhaging woman to the centurion's servant. So why does my five-year-old niece, Kelly, have brain cancer? Why did my brother-in-law abandon my sister and their family? Why does Daddy's arthritis not respond to medication?

There had to be something I wasn't seeing.

There had to be other reasons—good reasons beyond my under-standing—for God to allow such suffering.

Looking for Answers

I remember reading all the books on healing I could get my hands on. Gleaning counsel from friends and pastors and Christian lead-ers. Everyone agreed that God *could* heal any person any time, no matter how serious the problem.

But it was frustrating. No one could agree whether God *wills* to heal everybody who comes to Him in faith. Some said one thing, some said something else. And everyone seemed to back their posi-tions with Scripture.

For me, it all seemed to boil down into two extreme positions—with a plethora of opinions and positions in between. On the one hand, you have people who say healing was for "back then," that the age of miracles is past, and you shouldn't even ask for or expect healing today. After all, they will say, the book of Acts is just history … Luke's account is of a transitional era and not a guide for faith and practice today.

On the other side, you have people teaching that we can ap-propriate healing just like we do forgiveness of sins. They say that miracles ought to be part of the everyday life of the believer and that healing from disease is part of our heritage as sons and daughters of God.

They quote Isaiah 53:5, where it says that Messiah

> *was pierced for our transgressions,*
> *he was crushed for our iniquities;*
> *the punishment that brought us peace was upon him,*
> *and by his wounds we are healed.*

Or they will go to the book of 1 Peter, where it says, "He himself bore our sins in his body on the tree, so that we might die to sins and live for righteousness; by his wounds you have been healed" (1 Peter 2:24).

And then, as I said, you encounter every combination of those teachings imaginable. You have this theory and that theory. This interpretation and that interpretation. This person's experience and that person's experience.

I had my doubts about both extremes, but right from the get-go, I just couldn't go along with those who denied that God ever heals anyone miraculously today. In the first place, who is in a position to say this? Even if I didn't know of anyone whom God had healed in a way that defied medical explanation, what would that prove? It's a big wide world out there with people in every corner of it seeking the Lord with all their hearts.

In fact, I do know of such a person who was healed. A personal friend. A number of years ago, this mature Christian lady suffered from a severe bone-marrow disease. Every known medical procedure having failed, the doctors pronounced her "incurable" and advised her to get her affairs in order. There was no hope.

My friend, however, believes in the power of prayer. She and others simply took the matter before the Lord and placed it in His hands. When she returned to the doctor some time later for an examination, he dropped his jaw in amazement. This man was not a believer in Christ, but after taking repeated drug tests over a period of time, he told my friend. "There is no natural or medical explanation I can give. Your situation was beyond hope. All I can say is that this is a miracle."

Fifteen years later, she was still healthy. I knew this woman well enough to feel confident she was not deceiving me into believing something that never really happened.

Having related this story, however (and you probably have stories of your own), I have to say here that I really agree with people who insist on judging experiences by the light of Scripture, and not the other way around. Contemporary Christians tend to put too much weight on their experience anyway. Then they set up their conclusions as some kind of absolute truth by which everything else is to be interpreted, putting those experiences on an equal level with Scripture.

But this doesn't mean we should totally *ignore* our experiences. There are far too many all over the world who claim to have experienced or witnessed miraculous healing for us to write them off (which I would never do anyway). Many of these testimonies come from people who are soundly grounded in the Scriptures and mature in the faith—and many more are from the field of medicine. All of this should flash a yellow caution light in our minds if we're among those who feel the Bible totally rules out miracles for our day. It should make us go back and be sure we

God deals with His children as He wills.

have understood God's Word correctly. Here is a ruby, hard-won. God deals with His children as He wills. To one He gives a life of relative ease and comfort; to another He gives the privilege of suffering for Him in a concentration camp. For some, He rewards their faith in this life; for others, He waits until they step across the line into eternity. I can't take my own experience from the hand of God and set it up as the absolute norm for His dealing with others.

No, experiences aren't everything.

But they aren't nothing either.

So I had to rule out that pole of the spectrum that says God never heals miraculously today. In my opinion, the Bible doesn't teach it and experience doesn't support it.

All of this makes a lively debate in a Starbuck's over a cup of Caffé Verona. But it isn't theory when you have a teenager stricken with leukemia or a little one burning with fever or a spouse going blind. When you find yourself in the talons of fear over a loved one's medical report or submerged in an ocean of pain that won't recede and no medicine can touch, you probably won't be checking out an exhaustive theology book out of the library. You probably won't be dusting off your Bible school notes on dispensations and predestinations.

You'll probably be on your face before a living, loving God, crying out for His mercy. Suffering shrugs off academic arguments and sterile theological sub-points.

Suffering humbles us under the mighty hand of God.

So many of God's purposes remain shrouded in mystery to me ... and so they will until I begin a joyous "graduate study" in heaven. But I have learned some things ... rubies of wisdom I wish I could share with my younger self. Maybe the conversation would go like this:

I Wish I Were Healed

I know.

We wish for a lot of things. What's the old rhyme? If wishes were horses then beggars would ride. If wishes were reality, then the accident would have never happened, or if it had, I could get up out of my wheelchair and walk away from it forever. I could dance with my husband ... run into the California surf ... paint with my hands instead of my mouth ... walk down an autumn lane with wind in my hair and leaves crunching under my feet ... feel the strong body of a galloping horse beneath me ... cradle a newborn baby in my arms.

I recently became aware of a website where people from all over the world—including many who only have a working familiarity with English—post their wishes. Many of the wishes are lightweight, silly, or seem totally random. Like the one that said:

My wish is to collect $2,250 by 11/7/07.

Isn't that interesting? The wisher doesn't want $10,000, or even $2,249.99. The desired amount isn't a penny less or a penny more than $2,250. But as long as you're wishing, why not wish for a million?

Then there's the wisher who posted this modest desire:

I wish I become the most successful person in the world.

I've got to admire that one. He or she decided to push it to the max, to go for the biggest prize. But how will they know if their wish is ever granted? What is the criterion for worldly success? Money? Fame? Power? And would they really be happy if they "had it all"? Another anonymous wisher also longed for success—but with a touch more realism.

I wish to succeed in everything in my life, unfortunately I'm unsuccessful in everything.

One nameless woman who (for the moment) felt like a winner in the lottery of life, still felt compelled to wish that the happiness would never go away.

Now that I've finally found my one, I wish we'll be together and love one another forever. I wish we'll tie the knot soon and take care of each other for the rest of our lives. We belong to each other forever and will never fall apart.

A few of the wishes betray deep longings or unimaginable distress. "Emmi" wrote (to no one in particular):

I wish I could have a baby. Ever since I was little I have always wanted to have a child, and it seems to be the hardest thing in the world for me to achieve ...

Another woman sounded really desperate:

I wish I get well soon. I can't go for an another operation. God, please help me from my mother-in-law. I know, whatever dissatisfaction I have in my life, all for her ONLY!!! She brought me in this condition, where I find myself ill, not happy with anything. Because of this illness I can't have kids too and I know that was and is her wish. God, please help me, help me help me!!!

Was it a wish with God's name attached or a prayer? God only knows. When I read these postings I thought to myself, How sad! People wish for things with no real belief that their wishing will make any difference at all. It's an obvious exercise in futility, and yet they do it anyway, because ... what are we to do with all those deep longings in our heart? A wish may be only a coin tossed in a fountain, a four-leaf clover, or a helium balloon released into the wind ... but people want so much to be happy and don't know what else to do or where else to turn.

I could wish for a lot of things. I have, I do, and I suppose I always will. But wishes are whipped cream, cotton candy, and a wisp of steam off your morning coffee. There's nothing to them except a pleasant daydream that can occupy the imagination for a moment before dumping you back into an unhappy real world with nothing accomplished and no dreams fulfilled.

Children of God are all about reality, and don't have to live on wishes.

Hope is better than a wish.

The apostle Paul writes:

> Not only so, but we also rejoice in our sufferings, because we know that suffering produces perseverance; perseverance, character; and character, hope. *And hope does not disappoint us,* because God has poured out his love into our hearts by the Holy Spirit, whom he has given us. (Romans 5:3–5, emphasis added)

Wishes tie us to fantasies with wispy, spiderweb filaments. Hope ties us to the reality of the living God and the changeless truth of His Word with tugboat cable as thick as an old growth cedar.

As I've mentioned, there was a period in my life when I couldn't face my true situation and wanted to stay in bed all day living in a fantasy world, pretending my accident had never happened. That path, as Solomon tells us so vividly, would eventually lead to death, not life.

> *There is a way that seems right to a man,*
> *but in the end it leads to death.*
>
> (Proverbs 14:12)

Life is short enough without investing it on flights-of-fancy and wishing-upon-a-star. When we come before our God, worn down by our sorrows and disabilities as we may be, we come before a real and all-powerful Lord who loves us.

The book of Hebrews, addressed to a discouraged company of believers enduring the fires of persecution, is full of words of strong encouragement. Speaking of the promises God has given us as His children, the author reminds us that

> we who have fled to take hold of the hope offered to us may be greatly encouraged. We have this hope as an anchor for the soul, firm and secure. It enters the inner sanctuary behind the curtain, where Jesus, who went before us, has entered on our behalf. (Hebrews 6:18–20)

The hope that God offers has nothing in common with "wishing upon a star." The hope that ties us to Jesus and to heaven is the strongest hope in the universe. Biblical hope doesn't say, "I wish," it says, *"I know."*

And even though our circumstances here on earth may be terribly difficult—or even overwhelming—God has given us something, Someone, to hang onto until He steps in to change our situation or take us home.

The bottom line? God wants us to live in reality, not fantasyland. In the J. B. Phillips paraphrase, Paul says to the Romans: "As I think you have realized, the present time is of highest importance —it is time to wake up to reality. Every day brings God's salvation nearer. The night is nearly over, the day has almost dawned" (Romans 13:11 – 12).

But Why Wasn't I Healed?

Is it because God has changed?

A million times no.

Is God still the God of miracles and wonders in this present age?

A million times yes.

He operates in the natural and in the supernatural with equal ease. He is as powerful and as present and as attentive today as He has ever been.

> *Surely the arm of the LORD is not too short to save,*
>   *nor his ear too dull to hear. . . .*
>
> (Isaiah 59:1)

> *The LORD your God is with you,*
>   *he is mighty to save.*
>
> (Zephaniah 3:17)

Miracles of healing still happen. But they are not the everyday rule-of-thumb.

Many eyes will stay blind. Many babies will die at birth. Many cancers will not be eradicated until that ultimate healing of a new body and a new life in His presence. And many paraplegics and quadriplegics will never regain the use of unresponsive legs, arms, and hands.

As a ruby I would love to share with my younger self. I would gently say, "Joni, no matter how much we may wish it were otherwise, the Bible does not teach that He will always heal those who come to Him in faith. He sovereignly reserves the right to heal or not to heal as He sees fit. He sovereignly reserves the right to call His children home to heaven at the moment of His choosing."

Even when the God-Man walked the earth only a small number of people — those who happened to be in His immediate vicinity — were healed. He fed five thousand and He fed four thousand but many in Israel were still hungry. He drove out demons wherever He went, but He never went very far, and many demons remained entrenched, most likely to this very day in that tortured, blood-soaked land. He raised several from the dead, but only a few, who would live a few more years to die yet again.

Look at the first chapter of Mark's gospel. After word spread throughout Capernaum about Jesus healing Simon's mother-in-law, the whole town brought their sick and lame and gathered outside Simon's home. Long after sunset, Jesus was still healing people with infirmities and illnesses. The next day, very early in the morning, the people returned, bringing more friends and relatives who needed healing.

But Jesus was nowhere around.

Simon and his companions went to look for Him, and when they found Him off in a solitary place praying, they exclaimed, "Everyone is looking for you!"

You would think Jesus would jump to His feet, gather up His robe and go running down the hill. Not so. Reading Mark 1:38, you can almost picture Him rising slowly to His feet, dusting off His robe, then replying after a moment's thought, "Let us go somewhere else — to the nearby villages — so I can preach there also. That is why I have come."

It's not that He stopped caring about the cancer-ridden and the blind and the lame; it's just that their illnesses weren't His primary focus. The Gospel was. His main message was, sins kill, hell is real, but God is merciful. His kingdom will change you, and I am your passport. Whenever people missed this — whenever they started coming to Him to have their pains and problems removed — Jesus backed away.

No matter how great our faith or fervent our prayers, there will be times—perhaps many times—when our plea for health and healing will be answered with no.

But not everyone agrees with that.

A couple of years ago I agreed to a guest appearance with a well-known Christian television icon. After a number of minutes of carefully sharing my views on healing and God's will, the host turned to the camera and said, "Brothers and sisters, we shouldn't allow ourselves to be duped by Satan in these matters. Healing is promised in God's Word, and it really all boils down to a matter of your faith."

By implication, he was telling a national television audience that the reason I sat there beside him in a wheelchair was because I didn't have faith. Or at least not *enough*. Had he never read all the times God specifically tells His followers—even followers with great faith—to expect hardship? Second Corinthians 1:5 says, "The sufferings of Christ flow over into our lives," and Acts 14:22 warns us we must go through many hardships to enter the kingdom of God. And that's just scratching the surface!

Still, I was stung by those unexpected remarks, and I felt my face growing hot with hurt and indignation. It was all I could do to wait for a commercial break before tears flowed from my eyes.

The man may have a huge ministry and millions of viewers, but He is wrong. God is God, and it is He and He alone who decides who will be healed and who will not. Yes, faith is vital to everything, and "without faith it is impossible to please Him." But faith's focus must always be Jesus Christ—and nobody draws close to Christ who doesn't first share in Christ's sufferings. Besides, at the end of the day, it is not who has the most faith, but what God in His wisdom, love, and sovereignty chooses to do.

Who Causes My Trials? God or Satan?

The LORD said to Satan, "Very well, then, everything he has
is in your hands, but on the man himself do not lay a finger."

> Then Satan went out from the presence of the LORD. (Job 1:12)

The words were scarcely out of God's mouth when Sabeans massacre Job's servants, lightning kills sheep and shepherds, Chaldeans slaughter camels and herdsmen, and a desert wind collapses a house on Job's children.

How tragic!

Yet in a nutshell, Job's saga teaches us everything we need to know about God's sovereignty. (And maybe a nutshell is about all we could really handle anyway.)

What caused Job's trials? At the most basic level, *natural forces* did — natural low-pressure systems that could have been explained in scientific terms. At the same basic level, *evil people* caused Job's trials — those greedy raiding parties needed no prompting; they devised their own wicked schemes. At a deeper level, *Satan* did — the Devil turned around after leaving God's presence, and before we can blink, carnage is everywhere. Scripture leaves little doubt that Satan was behind instigating those roaming cutthroats and sponsoring those killer storms. (Although the storms were a natural phenomena and the pillagers acted in a way natural to violent men, the Bible says Satan engineered it all.)

So who or what caused Job's trials? At the deepest level, *the adversity in Job's life came about through God's rule and authority over everything.* Yes, Satan had asked permission to stir things up, but ultimately, it was God who signed the authorization papers.

Satan, in his hatred for God and humanity, acted freely according to his nature.

The bloodthirsty Sabeans behaved like, well, bloodthirsty Sabeans.

The Chaldeans fell into their normal pattern of wickedness.

And the freak storms behaved according to natural laws. If Job's kids would have had the Weather Channel in those days, they could have seen it coming on satellite images or Doppler radar.

God's overarching plan made room for Job's trials, but God didn't cause them. God exploited the deliberate evil of some bad characters and the impersonal evil of some bad storms without forcing anyone's hand.

We're faced with the same dilemma centuries later, when Moses stood in the presence of Pharaoh, king of Egypt. In the space of two chapters, the Bible tells us:

> But this time also Pharaoh hardened his heart and would not let the people go. (Exodus 8:32)

And then we read ...

> But the LORD hardened Pharaoh's heart, and he would not let the Israelites go. (Exodus 10:20)

So which is it? Who did the hardening of Pharaoh's heart? As God's ambassador to the Egyptian king, Moses went before Pharaoh's royal throne more than once to say, "Let my people go!"

Yet Pharaoh was immovable; his heart had been hardened against the Israelites. But when it comes to Pharaoh's stony resolve and exactly *who* did the hardening, Scripture points to both Pharaoh and the Lord.

A collaboration leading to evil?

No, that cannot be. We know from James 1:13 that God does not inject the idea of evil into anyone's heart. So how is it that "the Lord hardened Pharaoh's heart"?

Through the common work of grace in our world, God is constantly staving off evil and restraining the fury of Satan so that harm and calamity do not overwhelm us. In the final analysis, the devil can only do what God allows. Every once in awhile, however—as in the case of Pharaoh—God lifts His hand of restraining grace to allow evil men to carry out their wicked plans, *only* as it serves God's higher purposes.

God was as much as saying to Pharaoh, "So you want to sin?

You're determined to defy Me and close your mind and heart to My voice and to the miraculous evidence before your very eyes? Very well, then. You've chosen your course. You've made your bed, and now you will sleep in it. But I will make sure that when you do, your evil intentions suit My higher purposes and plan. You will defy Me for now, but soon—and too late—you will see My glory."

I'm reminded of the much-quoted statement of C. S. Lewis: "There are two kinds of people: those who say to God, 'Thy will be done,' and those to whom God says, 'All right, then, have it your way.'"

Solomon tells us:

> *A man who remains stiff-necked*
> *after many rebukes*
> *will suddenly be destroyed*
> *—without remedy.*
>
> (Proverbs 29:1)

And that certainly was the case with Pharaoh. He was allowed to go his evil, reckless way—but even in his wickedness, God would turn the evil the king intended into salvation for His people.

Even though humans have an intellect and a will of their own, God ultimately governs all they do—including evil intentions. And He does it *all* without impugning His righteous and holy character.

In other words, God doesn't say, "Into each life a little rain must fall" and then aim a hose in earth's general direction to see who gets the wettest. Rather He screens the trials that come to each of us, allowing only those that accomplish His good plans. He takes no joy in human agony. Nothing happens by accident, not even tragedy, not even sins committed against us. God is in control, and that's what I love about Him.

True, God's decrees allow suffering, but He doesn't "do" the suffering. He's not the one wielding the club.

These are deep waters, my friend.

Welcome to the world of finite humans trying to comprehend an infinite God. As we've said, God permits all sorts of things He doesn't approve of. He allows others to do what He would never do.

He didn't steal Job's camels.

He didn't entice the blood-thirsty Sabeans to wreak havoc.

He didn't push the four pillars of the house down on a joyous family dining together.

And yet ... He didn't take His hand off the wheel for thirty seconds, either.

This idea doesn't sit well with many people. But think of the alternative. What if God insisted on a hands-off policy toward the tragedies swimming your way? What if He removed all of the restraints from Satan? Left to his own, the Devil would make Jobs out of all of us.

But God curbs evil. Evil can only raise its head where God deliberately backs away — always for reasons that are specific, wise, and good — but often hidden during this present life.[10]

So (and here's the big question): *Who caused my diving accident?*

I could ask, "Was it God's fault?" and be assured that although He is sovereign, no it was not His fault.

I might wonder ... *Was my accident a direct attack from the devil?*

Well, yes, maybe it was. But I could press that still further and say that it was neither a direct assault from God or the devil, but simply the consequence of living in a fallen world fraught with dangers (like a shifting sandbar in the shallow water of Chesapeake Bay).

The point is, I never did rise up out of my wheelchair after the little prayer meeting in that country church. But God was there. He was listening with tender compassion. He was lovingly holding the entire moment in His powerful and sovereign hands.

Do your circumstances seem to be careening out of control? Remember that God is with you through it, loving you and caring

... and allowing the details to play out exactly in accordance with His plan.

When life seems wild, crazy, and utterly out of control, it is not.

When it seems as though God has forgotten you or turned His back on you to tinker with some other universe, He has not.

When it seems like you have somehow fallen out of His favor, been edged outside the circle of His protection, or missed the bus on His love, you have not.

And that's what it means to walk by faith.

10

Behind Enemy Lines

It's quiet around the house this afternoon. In an hour or so, the yellow school bus will drop off my niece Kay. Jay's outside in the garden, mothering her zucchinis and radishes. I can see her through the bay window of my drawing studio.

No friends, no visitors today. I have the place to myself. It's kind of lonely.

Over on the corner of the desk, there's a book I've been wanting to read. It looks just within nudging reach. That means positioning my arm by the book and manipulating it toward me, through awkward jerking motions.

Great idea, but there's a problem. The book is just on the borderline of being out of reach. I'll have to stretch ... get my wrist beside it ... try to pull it my way without knocking it off the desk altogether. Maybe I can zigzag it. My cousin Eddie once taught me about sailing into a headwind and how you had to tack back and forth, back and forth to make progress. So I'm tacking the book. Left a little. Right a little. Inching it toward me.

I'm not sure I'll ever get used to failing at tasks that even people with disabilities can usually accomplish. That book. It's about an inch and a half farther away than I'm used to reaching. I can move it—but not toward me. Come on, book! Cooperate! Every nudge seems to push it farther away. My only hope is to try to press the weight of my arm downward on top of the cover and attempt a quick jerk back toward me.

And there it goes. Off the table onto the floor. It's within eight inches of my dangling arm, and I can't touch it. I could yell for Jay, but she's way out there, happy in her garden. She'd never hear. Anyway, I'm tired of yelling for Jay. Tired of people having to do everything for me. Tired of feeling so helpless.

How I wish I had my hands back. I think I'd even be satisfied to stay paralyzed from the waist down ... *but I want my hands!*

Tears of frustration now. And no one to wipe my face or help me blow my nose.

I'm trying so hard to keep this in perspective, trying to see my life as You do. But oh dear God ... I still want to be healed.

FORTY YEARS LATER
I HAVE TO REFLECT ...

Is Keeping a Right Perspective Really Worth It?

Is the perseverance worth the heartache?

Is the bleeding worth the benefit?

Is a tenacious faith worth the price tag of heartache?

Yes! More than we can possibly realize. Let me quote this passage one more time: "Our light and momentary troubles are achieving for us eternal glory that far outweighs them all" (2 Corinthians 4:17).

What heaven knows is pleasures and joys, the ecstasy and the elation. As far as heaven is concerned, our troubles are "light" in comparison. This is another verse written in end-time perspective, telling us, "This is the way it will turn out; this is the way it will be—you'll see!" Again, it's a matter of faith. A pile of problems are on one side of the scale; heaven's glory, the other.

After forty years of extreme disability, I can testify that my trials seem anything but "light" or "momentary." If the Holy Spirit hadn't used the words Himself in God's infallible Word, I would have never, ever used such terms to describe my condition.

But if *He* says my paralysis has been a light affliction, and just a temporary, passing, soon-to-be-forgotten phase, then I will stand on that promise while I still have breath. And I will continue to allow my anticipation of that future "eternal glory" to backlight all of the difficult days of my journey on this side of heaven.

Yes, we all have "those mornings," don't we?

Sometimes we get up and almost from the start everything seems to go wrong. When it comes to my morning routine, just getting me ready for a normal day takes a great amount of effort—for me and my helpers. And then there are those inevitable physical complications of my paralysis that make the process that much slower and take even longer!

We all have our hard days and forgettable moments. But let's just imagine that you find yourself enduring the worst morning you can remember. I'm not talking about spilling the coffee or burning the toast or having an argument with your teenager or getting stuck in a monster traffic jam. What I mean are events that could utterly devastate you, casting a deep shadow over your marriage, your health, your children, your finances, your dreams, or your nearest and dearest friendships.

You might find yourself wondering, "How can I survive the day? How can I make it through? How can I go on?"

But as long as we're imagining, then picture this: someone you trust completely gives you an ironclad promise that by later that day, sometime in the afternoon, your serious issue will be resolved and you will find yourself full of joy and having the time of your life. Wouldn't that change your perspective? Wouldn't that give you the courage to hold on and walk through the hours of that difficult day?

I often think of the thief dying on a cross alongside the Lord Jesus in His darkest hour. This man, beyond all argument, was having the worst morning of his life.

He had just been crucified.

The only thing he had to "look forward to" was a terrible death, and an ultimate release from his agony. But that was untold hours away. In the meantime, he had to undergo one of the cruelest and most barbaric forms of torture ever devised by evil men.

What an end to a miserable, unhappy life! In his unspeakable pain and great bitterness of spirit, he lashed out at the closet person to him.

Who happened to be the Son of God, possibly mere feet away.

> "You bragged that you could tear down the Temple and then rebuild it in three days—so show us your stuff!... He saved others—He can't save himself! The Messiah of God—ha! The Chosen—ha!" (Matthew 27:40; Luke 23:35 THE MESSAGE)

But something happened as those awful minutes and hours slipped by. Somehow, right in the worst of it, a shutter flicked open in the doomed man's soul, and it came to his mind that salvation might be only inches away from him.

As the other crucified felon kept cursing and heaping insults on Jesus, this man suddenly turned on the mocker.

> "Have you no fear of God? You're getting the same as him. We deserve this, but not him—he did nothing to deserve this." (Luke 23:41 THE MESSAGE)

And then, in those last few hours, the thief on the cross did the best thing he'd ever done in his brief, wretched life. He cast his lot on Jesus Christ.

> "Jesus, remember me when you come into your kingdom."
> Jesus answered him, "I tell you the truth, today you will be with me in paradise." (Luke 23:42–43)

When would he be in paradise with Jesus? *Today*. If, as some have calculated, this conversation took place around ten in the morning and Jesus died at three in the afternoon, this repentant man would have to suffer for at least five more hours. The pain didn't go away. The searing agony didn't relent. From all appearances, his situation hadn't changed at all.

But in reality, *everything* had changed. Because he now possessed something he had not possessed — or even imagined possessing — when this worst-of-all days dawned for him.

He started with a death sentence, but now he had a promise. And such a promise! *Today . . . Jesus . . . Paradise*. The worst of horrors now offered the best prospect imaginable. Every minute of suffering thrust him nearer to a radiant ocean of happiness. The approaching door of death would open to a forever-new life.

If the problem side of life's scale seems intolerably heavy to you right now, then focus your faith on the glory side.

That's not denial or escapism. It is rock-solid reality. God wants us to think about the Life to come. Why else would He give us such tantalizing glimpses of what lies ahead for us? Thinking about heaven, God's presence, and future glory won't distract or detract from our life and responsibilities here on earth; it will *equip* us to live and respond to life with a better perspective.

When you reserve some of your thoughts and a portion of your day to pondering heaven, you're a Rumpelstiltskin weaving straw into gold; like a divine spinning wheel, your affliction "*worketh . . . a far more exceeding and eternal weight of glory*" (2 Corinthians 4:17 KJV, emphasis added). Or as J. B. Phillips paraphrases: "These little troubles (which are really so transitory) are winning for us a permanent, glorious and solid reward out of all proportion to our pain."

It's not merely that heaven will be wonderful *in spite* of our anguish; it will be wonderful *because* of it.

Here, my friends, is a ruby of wisdom, hard-won: a faithful

response to affliction and hardship and pain accrues a *weight* of glory.

God has every intention of rewarding your endurance. A bounteous reward. Why else would He meticulously chronicle every one of your tears?

> *Record my lament;*
>   *list my tears on your scroll—*
>   *are they not in your record?*
>   (Psalm 56:8)

Every tear you've cried—think of it—will be redeemed. God will give you indescribable glory for your grief. Not with a general wave of the hand, but in a considered and specific way. Each tear has been listed; each will be recompensed. We know how valuable our tears are in his sight—when Mary anointed Jesus with the valuable perfume, it was her tears with which she washed his feet that moved Him powerfully. (See Luke 7:44.)

The worth of our weeping is underscored again in Revelation 21:4 where "he will wipe every tear from their eyes." It won't be the duty of angels or the task of elders with golden crowns. It will be God's.

It's not merely that heaven will be wonderful in spite of our anguish; it will be wonderful because of it.

"Weeping may endure for a night, but joy cometh in the morning" (Psalm 30:5 KJV).

Our reward will be our joy. The more faithful to God we are in the midst of pain, the more reward and joy. The gospels are packed with parables of kings honoring servants for their diligence, landlords showering bonuses on faithful laborers, monarchs placing loyal subjects in charge of many cities. Whatever suffering you are going through this minute, your reaction to it affects the eternity you will enjoy. And that makes *every* moment of our pain and hardship laden with opportunity and alive with possibility.

White Stones and Hidden Manna

Heaven will be more heavenly to the degree that you have followed Christ on earth. Paul wrote, "I consider that our present sufferings are not worth comparing with the glory that will be revealed in us" (Romans 8:18).

It has been said that something so grand, so glorious is going to happen in the world's finale—something so awesome and wonderful—the dénouement of the Lord Jesus—that it will suffice for every hurt, it will compensate for every inhumanity, and it will atone for every terror. His glory will fill the universe and hell will be an afterthought compared to the resplendent brightness of God's cosmos and "the Lamb who gives light" (Revelation 21:23 paraphrased).

Can you even begin to conceive of these things?

You take that step through time and space and put down your feet on heaven's court. You drop to your knees to express thanks and gratitude. The Man of Sorrows walks from His throne and approaches you. He has absolutely no doubt of your appreciation, for He knows you have suffered. He reaches toward you with His nail-scarred hands, and you feel your hands in His. You are not embarrassed. Your own scars, your anguish, all those times you felt rejection and pain, have given you at least a tiny taste of what the Savior endured to purchase your redemption. Your suffering, like nothing else, has prepared you to meet God—for what proof could you have brought of your love if this life left you totally unscarred?

You have something eternally precious in common with Christ—suffering! But to your amazement, the fellowship of sharing in His suffering has faded like a half-forgotten dream. Now it is a fellowship of sharing in His joy and presence. Pleasure made somehow more wonderful by earthly years of pain.

Oh, the pain of earth, you half sigh. Then you smile, rising to your feet to live the life God had been preparing for you all along. Weeping may have endured for a night, but it is morning.

The joy has come.

And so will the rewards.

In the book of Revelation, the last book of the Bible, the resurrected Christ hands out warnings, rebukes, words of commendation, and promises of reward to seven churches in Asia. Whatever else Bible commentators see in those letters (and trust me, they see a lot), you can't miss one strong theme: Jesus commends believing men and women who have shown the faith, courage, and perseverance to continue walking with Him and trusting Him in the midst of devastating trials.

And His rewards are more than just a handshake and a "well done." There are specific, wonderful, incomprehensible rewards that He will personally present to those who have remained faithful "through it all."

To the one who is faithful, to the one who overcomes ...

... I will give the right to eat from the tree of life, which is in the paradise of God.

... I will give you the crown of life. He who overcomes will not be hurt at all by the second death.

... I will give some of the hidden manna. I will also give him a white stone with a new name written on it, known only to him who receives it.

... I will give authority over the nations ... I will also give him the morning star.

... I will make a pillar in the temple of my God. Never again will he leave it. I will write on him the name of my God and the name of the city of my God, the new Jerusalem, which is coming down out of heaven from my God; and I will also write on him my new name.

... I will give the right to sit with me on my throne, just as I overcame and sat down with my Father on his throne. (See Revelation 2–3.)

Do these rewards apply to all believers who suffer with courage and perseverance? Maybe, maybe not. Who can say? But the fact is, He *will* reward His redeemed people. Paul writes "that the Lord will reward each one of us for the good we do, whether we are slaves or free" (Ephesians 6:8 NLT). And in some of those beautiful closing words of Scripture, Jesus Himself says, "Behold, I am coming soon! My reward is with me, and I will give to everyone according to what he has done" (Revelation 22:12).

A crown of life . . . a tree of life . . . hidden manna . . . a white stone . . . the morning star. What are these things? What do they imply? They are as tantalizing and mysterious as resplendently wrapped presents under the Christmas tree. But we know this much: When the Almighty King of the cosmos wants to honor, bless, and lavish His love upon His faithful servants, He knows how to do it.

Why Doesn't God Do Something about Suffering?

He has. And He will.

God did not wash His hands of the earth and walk away in disgust. He did not give up on His creation and chalk it up as a failed attempt.

For one thing, God cannot fail.

For another thing, God—in His very nature—is a Redeemer. If God were to totally wipe out suffering, He would have to eradicate all sin. And the inconvenient truth about that fact is that it would also mean He'd have to get rid of all sinners at the same time. Thankfully, there's too much redemptive love in God to do that!

Way back in the book of Genesis—while sin was still a fresh, ugly wound on His beautiful Creation—He promised that one day a Redeemer would come who would deal both with sin and with sin's results . . . with the curse, and with those who have been harmed by the curse. The whole Old Testament foreshadows this coming One, and as its pages unfold, pictures of this coming Messiah become increasingly clear.

When Jesus died on the cross and God raised Him from the dead, He served notice that Satan's vise-grip hold on the earth was broken, that God had opened the door to full reconciliation through the cross. It is now only a matter of time before He will return as a Warrior and Conquering King, to overthrow evil forever, heal every hurt, and right every wrong.

"Only a matter of time" ... yet that time is not yet.

"I am coming soon," He says again and again. But the day hasn't arrived.

We still camp on enemy soil. We still live in an era when the evil one is "roaming through the earth and going back and forth in it" (Job 1:7). When the Bible calls Satan the "prince of this world" (John 12:31) and "the ruler of the kingdom of the air" (Ephesians 2:2), when it acknowledges that "the whole world is under the control of the evil one" (1 John 5:19), it means what it says.

We can sing, "This is my Father's world, He shines in all that's fair," and be right—up to a point. He created the world and all its beauty. He paid the price to redeem the world. And He will certainly return to throw out the present evil "tenant," and cleanse every vestige of his cruel occupation. But for now, "this is [Satan's] hour—when darkness reigns" (Luke 22:53).

When Jesus came the first time, as the God-man and Messiah, He laid the foundation for His rule. He established a beachhead for the kingdom of heaven, and there will be those times, those situations, where He rolls back the curse in the life of one of His children. But the world is still broken. The King has not yet come to rule and reign. And the devil knows his time is short.

Paul reminds us to

> be strong in the Lord and in his mighty power.... For our struggle is not against flesh and blood, but against the rulers,

against the authorities, against the powers of this dark world and against the spiritual forces of evil in the heavenly realms. (Ephesians 6:10, 12)

There are powers of evil that make this world a dark place, spiritually. Since our eyes have adjusted to the darkness since birth, we probably don't even realize how shadowed and dim our world truly is. When the Bible gives accounts of the occasional appearances of angels, arriving on earth directly from heaven, the writers will often speak of the almost blinding brightness of these servants of God.

His body looked like a precious gem. His face flashed like lightning, and his eyes like flamed torches. His arms and feet shone like polished bronze. (Daniel 10:6 NLT)

His appearance was like lightning, and his clothes were white as snow. (Matthew 28:3)

Two men in clothes that gleamed like lightning stood beside them. (Luke 24:4)

The other day my friend Doug was telling me about an old movie theater he used to frequent when he was a boy. It was strange in that it had no lobby. You walked through the glass doors, and within a few feet you would pass through a curtain and bump up against the back row. When the movie was over, there was no vestibule to ease you out of darkness and back into daylight. He described how kids would walk outside, rub their eyes, and almost bump into lampposts — the light was a jolt to their senses.

Doug added, "I almost forgot about that theater until I read 1 Peter 2:9." When I asked him to explain the connection, he said, "As a Christian, I forget what a blinding jolt it was to be taken out of darkness and placed in light."

He's right. We Christians can hardly recall the blinding reality of being translated from the kingdom of darkness to the kingdom of God's dear Son. One minute we were heading to hell; the next, heaven. One minute we were dead in our sins; the next, alive unto

God. If we really thought about it, we would be overwhelmed, rubbing our eyes and explaining, "What a jolt *this* is!"

That's a reminder how light and dazzling and radiant it was when God walked the pathways of Eden with His friends, Adam and Eve … and again how it will be when Jesus finally sits on the throne of a cleansed and renewed earth. But until that day, until He takes us home or returns as conquering King, we will live in the half light of a world yet to be fully redeemed. Our address will still read: "Behind enemy lines."

Jesus has come … and He is coming.

Now … He invades behind enemy lines in daring raids. And if you could be up above the world looking down through the spiritual darkness shrouding our planet, you would see starbursts of light all over the world—like flashbulbs in a darkened auditorium. **Then** … will "the clouds be rolled back as a scroll."

Now … in His mercy He brings healings here and there, touching this life and that. **Then** … He will banish even the memory of illness or pain or death forever.

Now … He gives grace to endure, strength to persevere, patience to wait, and the immediate presence of His Spirit to comfort. **Then** … the waiting will be over, and He will give us our heart's every desire.

Now … He gives us rubies of wisdom in exchange for our suffering and long endurance in His name. **Then** … "the earth will be filled with the knowledge of the glory of the LORD, as the waters cover the sea" (Habakkuk 2:14).

But Why Would He Say No to My Healing?

It's not because He lacks ability.

It's not because He lacks concern.

It's not because He is deficient in love.

It's not because He is somehow preoccupied and has forgotten about us.

As the years have gone by, I have pondered many of the answers frequently given to the "whys" of suffering.

Know God better through suffering? That's a quaint thought. Then again, there's that high school buddy who never did take God seriously until trouble hit. Bagging a football scholarship to a Big Ten university consumed all his attention, but in his sophomore year at Nebraska, he got slammed on the five-yard line. Two surgeries and three sidelined seasons later, he had done some serious thinking. Life was short ... where were his priorities? Today, he is still into sports (he coaches the Tiny Tornadoes after work). But his priorities are straighter. Bible study and prayer get their chunk of time on his schedule.

Closer to God through trials? Another curiosity. Then there is the couple down the street who tend to be just a tad materialistic. But last year when he lost his job, he prayed harder, got by with less, and learned some lessons. They discovered that family means more than possessions, that community college wasn't so bad for their Princeton-bound daughter, and that God took care of them while they climbed back on their feet.

Discover God's hand in heartbreak? One more peculiarity. But then there's the twenty-six-year-old man whose girlfriend had returned the engagement ring. He let it sit on his dresser for months as a monument to his failed love life. He dealt with his grief by pouring himself into a troubled kid who lived two doors down and had never known a father. Took him to the stables on weekends and taught him to ride horseback. It made the jilted young man grow up. He learned that his problems were super-small.

Two years later the man ducked into a bookstore to buy a present and spied a honey-blonde girl with a knock-out smile flipping through a calendar of palomino horses. They got to talking and discovered they had more in common than just equines. He took her riding the next weekend, joined the singles group at her church, and not long afterward, she said a big yes when he popped the question on her front porch swing. Today, he shudders to think that he could have missed her.

Why would He say no to our cry for healing and relief from suffering? The full answer to that question — and most of our questions — is hidden in mystery, and may never be revealed in this life. Even so, the Bible shows us again and again that an Almighty God gains glory when His hurting, broken, sons and daughters continue to love and trust and praise Him in the midst of heartbreak and loss.

The fact is, you and I can praise God and exalt Christ in all of life, when we are healthy, strong, wealthy, and at the top of our game, or when we have been so deeply wounded and crushed by hardships that we feel weak as a little child.

But it is in the latter circumstances, that both men and angels take notice.

Let's return just for a moment to a story we considered in Chapter 2: that of Paul and Silas's unjust imprisonment in Acts 16. Change just a few variables in that story, and the ending would have been vastly different. Their preaching could have been met with benign indifference by the public officials, and every door could have swung open for them and their message in that city. Who wouldn't choose that outcome over the one these loyal servants of God had to endure?

Have you ever been arrested? Not just given a ticket on the side of the freeway, but actually apprehended, cuffed, stuffed into the back of a squad car, hauled into a police station, and then photographed and fingerprinted? How would you feel if the police came for you while you were in church, taking you by both arms and escorting you down the aisle toward the exit, while everyone gaped and stared at you? Would that be just a little humiliating? Even if you knew you had committed no crime, think of the conversations in homes and restaurants after church that Sunday. Think of the rumors and the sad nodding of heads: "I always kind of wondered about him. . . . . Something about her seemed just a little odd to me. Well you never know, do you?"

Do you think being falsely accused and arrested was any less humiliating for Paul and Silas, these godly missionaries?

The text says that they were then ordered to be "stripped and beaten." In fact, "severely flogged." I wouldn't want any part of such a thing. Stripped in front of the crowd? That's what the text says, and it would have been mortifying. Then severely flogged? Having people watch while the skin is flayed off your back and sides, exposing muscle tissue while your own blood flowed for the sick pleasure of a sadistic mob? What a ghastly thing to happen—to anyone!

Then, they were thrown into prison—in a dark, putrid inner cell—and forced into an agonizing position in crude wooden stocks while their heads spun with shock and nausea.

Who would volunteer for that kind of horror? Who would sign up for humiliation, injustice, and slashing, fiery pain? Wouldn't it have been immeasurably better if the city officials had greeted their message with a yawn and a shrug of the shoulders, allowing the missionaries to establish a new base in the province?

Yes. Of course.

But then ... the prisoners in the deep dungeons would have never wondered at praise rising to God from two men in stocks who had been beaten within an inch of their lives. And the jailer and his family would have continued their pagan lives and died in their sins. And God would have *never* supernaturally opened the prison doors with an earthquake—a divine intervention so powerful that the aftershocks of that earthquake have rumbled on for two millennia.

In the same way, Mary's vial of priceless perfume could have remained on a household shelf, covered with a fine layer of dust rather than being broken open and poured on the Lord Jesus. It could have become a family heirloom, treasured, protected, and passed from generation to generation.

But then ... Jesus would have gone to the cross with no lingering scent of a godly woman's sacrificial love, and Mary's story would have never been told to countless millions in numberless languages and dialects all over the world.

There is something about maintaining a faith-filled, positive attitude toward life in the midst of tragic events that takes a simple testimony and pushes it over the top. There is something about a song of praise rising out of brokenness that opens an artesian well of life.

Friend, if we can hang onto God for dear life when we are in the midst of a deep affliction, nothing—absolutely *nothing*—could be more powerful. For then we are showing God to be massively and supremely worthy of our trust and confidence despite the suffering.

So why do believers go through hardship, sorrow, and suffering? One reason is because God's name is lifted high when we honor Him through our tears. It is a "sacrifice of praise" to Him, that brings pleasure to His heart.

And it is powerful.

Divine Chemistry

Let me put it like this: I'm no chemist, but bear with me for a moment.

There is a particular chemistry unique to our planet, a blending of two fundamental elements creating an incomparable and irreversible transformation. In ordinary chemistry (I am told) such reactions occur with the fusion of particular electron configurations.

But never mind the electrons. In *this* chemistry, the reaction takes place with the blending of two seemingly irreconcilable human experiences. It is an outcome unique to this temporary life of ours on a broken planet, and it can never be duplicated in the age to come.

The two elements are *suffering* and *joy*.

When severe suffering and spontaneous joy mingle in a human soul in the same moment, something powerful results ... and the resulting reaction ripples through time, space, and beyond into eternity. All who see it are caught up in wonder. And more people *do* see it than we might believe possible.

In normal human life, these two experiences are opposites. We all know that suffering brings sorrow, depression, anxiety. We all know that happy circumstances and blessings bring joy. It's true. That's the normal chemistry. But in Christ—and only in Him—two contradictory events can intermingle, releasing a fragrance and transforming power that lasts for years.

And that is supernatural chemistry.

Jesus Himself showed us how it was done at Calvary. In Hebrews 12:2, the New Testament writer says of Jesus that "for the joy set before him [he] endured the cross." In one paraphrase of Isaiah 53 we read that "Out of that terrible travail of soul, he'll see that it's worth it and be glad he did it" (v. 11 The Message).

The same over-the-top chemistry has been carried on through those who bear the name of Jesus. In his letter to the Corinthians, Paul held up the example of believers in a neighboring province. Speaking of the beaten-down, impoverished church in Macedonia, he marveled: "Out of the most severe trial, their overflowing joy and their extreme poverty welled up in rich generosity" (2 Corinthians 8:2).

Out of severe *trial* ... overflowing *joy*.

Out of extreme *poverty* ... rich *generosity* welling up and overflowing.

How is that possible? It has to be the life of the indwelling Jesus Christ, so much larger than our own lives that He spills out and brims over at every turn. But especially through our pain.

In another passage, Paul commended the infant church in Thessalonica, saying, "In spite of severe suffering, you welcomed the message with the joy given by the Holy Spirit" (1 Thessalonians 1:6).

And what resulted from that intermingling of suffering and joy?

"You became a model to all the believers in Macedonia and Achaia. The Lord's message rang out from you not only in Macedonia and Achaia—your faith in God has become known everywhere" (1 Thessalonians 1:7–8).

The message of salvation rang out, or *sounded out* from these joyful, suffering saints. In the Greek language, the word translated "rang out" literally means "to echo forth." It refers to the sounding of a loud trumpet, that echoes from place to place to place. The influence of these suffering, joyful believers reached far, far beyond any normal expectation. Through them and because of them, the message of salvation and life in Jesus echoed and reechoed through the hills and valleys of Greece.

Thessalonica was something of a crossroads in those days, with merchants, soldiers, and travelers passing through on their way to Macedonia, Achaia, and different parts of Greece. And somehow, in the mystery of God's providence, the story of a radiant band of hard-pressed believers in that city spread like ripples from a stone tossed into a still pond.

Why? Why did that happen?

Because believers who suffer with faith, perseverance, and joy create an echo effect, taking the message of Jesus so much farther than even they could imagine. Picture a shout in a great canyon, that bounces wall to wall, never losing strength, for countless miles and numberless years.

Frankly, not many lives will be used in such a way. Not many people will ever know such an impact. Many of us will simply walk the short path through this life with only brief highs and lows, and make our way into eternity.

And after we breathe our last ... as far as we know ... *that's it.* There will be no more opportunity to carry the message of salvation to a dying world, because that world will have been changed forever. There will be no lost souls to guide toward the Savior who loves them, because the doors to heaven and hell will be closed. And there will be no opportunity to experience the power of suffering mingled with joy, because there will be no more suffering.

Not ever.

Here is a ruby, hard-won. Why does God allow some of His deeply loved sons and daughters to go through trials of body and spirit? Because if they receive that suffering with faith and joy, that supernatural "chemical reaction" will supercharge the message of His Son's love. And the suffering one will have the privilege of a life impact that may keep echoing and echoing beyond their years.

Back in 1967 missionary Doug Nichols fell ill while serving in India and had to spend several months in a dingy tuberculosis sanitarium. While there, he tried to give gospel tracts to the patients and doctors, but no one would accept them. It was a dark time in Doug's life. He was sick, weak, lonely, and disappointed no one would listen to him.

One night around 2:00 a.m., Doug woke up coughing. Across the aisle, he noticed an old man trying to get out of bed to go to the bathroom. Too weak to stand, the man fell back into bed crying and exhausted. Although sick himself and as weak as he had ever been, Doug got out of bed and with a smile placed one arm under the patient's neck and the other under his legs. With all his strength he lifted the man and carried him

> *Why does God allow some of His deeply loved sons and daughters to go through trials ...? Because if they receive that suffering with faith and joy, that supernatural "chemical reaction" will supercharge the message of His Son's love.*

down the hall to the filthy, smelly washroom. Then the missionary carried him back to his bed.

"*Dhanyawaad.*" The old man smiled, rasping the Hindi word for thanks.

What happened the next morning was amazing. One of the other patients woke Doug up with a steaming cup of tea, making motions that he wanted a gospel tract. The other patients asked for the booklets. Even the nurses and a doctor asked for one. Over the next few days, several patients and staff gave their lives to Christ. The whole situation changed overnight because of Doug's sacrificial act in the middle of the night.

The power of the Good News is released in your life when you allow your weakness to showcase the awesome might and love of our Savior. When we serve Him and model Him in our suffering, we have opportunities to extend His salvation farther than we ever could in our strength.

Marching to Zion

Before the start of the workday at our Joni and Friends offices, we often begin by singing a hymn together. Today we sang a hymn by Isaac Watts that always gets my heart beating faster: "We're Marching to Zion."

> Come, we that love the Lord,
> And let our joys be known;
> Join in a song with sweet accord,
> Join in a song with sweet accord
> And thus surround the throne,
> And thus surround the throne.
>
> We're marching to Zion,
> Beautiful, beautiful Zion;
> We're marching upward to Zion,
> The beautiful city of God.

I may be paralyzed, but when I sing this hymn, I *feel* like marching. And I am! I'm heading for heaven, a step closer every minute, every hour, every day. I'm living my life here on earth as though eternity depended on it. And it truly does.

This is why the Bible says, "Consider it pure joy, my brothers, whenever you face trials of many kinds" (James 1:2).

It reminds us:

> It was good for me to be afflicted,
> so that I might learn your decrees.
> (Psalm 119:71)

For our light and momentary troubles are achieving for us an eternal glory that far outweighs them all. (2 Corinthians 4:17)

Not only so, but we also rejoice in our sufferings. (Romans 5:3)

The Bible constantly tries to get us to look at life this way—and the longer I live the more I see it. Scripture steadfastly tries to implant the perspective of the future into our present, like a voice counseling us, "This is the way it's going to all turn out. This is how it will all seem when it's over, a better way, I promise. Keep on marching!"

It's a view that separates what is lasting from what will fall by the wayside.

It's a view that reminds us that real Life is out ahead of us, just over the horizon, and that we're moving toward a destination.

It's a view that teaches us that wisdom gained through faith and perseverance is more precious than rubies.

Scripture can do no less. It only deals in realities, always underscoring the final results—the heart settled, the soul rejoicing, the glimpses of Zion through parting clouds ... through tears. Human nature gags on such a perspective. I remember a friend of mine who had just lost his wife to cancer. His grief was like a heavy blanket draped over his body. He couldn't see two inches beyond his sorrow. "When I try to think about going on without her," he said, "I have a picture of myself walking on the backside of the moon for the rest of my life."

That's grief talking. And we all understand that. Our earthbound perspective tries to rivet us to the pain of the present, blinding us to the realities of the future. Human nature would rather lick its wounds and sneer, "That's pie in the sky. The future doesn't count."

But it does count. And it has everything to do with this present moment. Tim Stafford writes:

Scripture can seem at times so blithely and irritatingly out of touch with reality, brushing past huge philosophical problems and personal agony. That is just how life is when you are looking from the end. Perspective changes everything. What seemed so important at the time has no significance at all.[11]

Time is slippery stuff, isn't it? The past always looks different than it did back when. Memory is selective. It chooses only a few highlights of lasting importance from all that happened. When we recall pain in the past, we do so with a perspective we simply didn't have going through it.

We didn't understand how it would all pan out.

In the middle of suffering we see only confusion. For me, it was a bizarre mix of tie-dyed-T-shirts, the smell of pot in the hallways of the state institution, and thoughts of suicide. If we were looking for roads that lead somewhere through the pain, we were doing just that — looking, not finding them.

But now, so many years later, I'm finally understanding. I have found the path. All because I see things differently.

It depends on our perspective — where in time we are looking from. When looking back on a heartache, the pain fades like a hazy memory. The trauma has dulled like an old photograph. Only the results survive, the things of lasting importance — like the good marriage, the successful career, or in my case, the acceptance of a wheelchair.

These are the events that rise and remain, like stepping-stones above raging waters. These are the things that carry us to the other side of suffering, to the place where we have a sense of "arrival," the place where we are more "us" than we were years earlier.

When we come through "the valley of the shadow of death," we are different people. Better, strong, wiser. It's what happens on the other side of our heartaches and trials. He "prepares a table before me in the presence of my enemies." Like me, back in that state hospital, wheeling placidly by a faded poster of a huge marijuana leaf.

He anoints "my head with oil; my cup overflows" with the satisfaction of surviving suffering with a smile (Psalm 23:4–5).

The Bible blatantly tells us to "rejoice in suffering" and "welcome trials as friends" because God wants us to step into the reality He has in mind for us, the only reality that ultimately counts. It requires gutsy faith to do so, but as we trust God, we move beyond the present into the future. In fact, we enter the very future God intends for us.

> Your new life, which is your real life—even though invisible to spectators—is with Christ in God. He is your life. When Christ (your real life, remember) shows up again on this earth, you'll show up, too—the real you, the glorious you. (Colossians 3:3 The Message)

Real life which is invisible.

That seems as impossible to comprehend as "rejoicing in suffering." But don't forget, "Faith is being sure of what we hope for and certain of what we do not see" (Hebrews 11:1). Like watching an old-fashioned Polaroid snapshot develop before your eyes, the "we" God intends us to be as a result of suffering emerges when we "welcome trials." "We share in his sufferings in order that we may also share in his glory ... the glory that will be revealed *in us*" (Romans 8:17, 18, emphasis added).

The future is straining to get out. To be revealed in us. We have seen the future and it is us—Christ in us and us in Christ. "*If*, indeed, we share in his sufferings."

As we do, our perspective is changed.

And if there is one thing my wheelchair has done for me, it has changed my perspective. One day I will arrive in heaven, look in my rearview mirror at earth and see that, yes, suffering made my faith more muscular ... jerked my thoughts and values right-side-up ... honed and shaped my character ... made me more sensitive to others who were hurting ... and birthed a ministry to disabled people around the world.

But best of all, my hardships have pushed me deeper into the arms of my wonderful Savior. In short, my suffering blessed me with a heavenly point of view. And I love it. I'm *passionate* about it.

This is what God wants—hearts burning with a passion for the future things, on fire for kingdom realities that are out of this world. God wants His people aflame with hope as we move day-by-day toward "the better country."

A "consider it pure joy" outlook affects the way we live on earth. Though we still suffer as we march toward Zion, we become cities on a hill, and lights on a lamp stand for all to see and take courage from that welcome radiance. People whose hearts are ignited for heaven make good inhabitants of earth.

And that's not all. We leave a fragrance as we march by.

Paul tells us, it is God "who always leads us in triumphal procession in Christ and through us spreads everywhere the fragrance of the knowledge of him" (2 Corinthians 2:14).

Suffering in the present turns our hearts toward the future, like a mother turning the face of her child, insisting, "Look *this* way!" Once heaven has our attention, a fervid anticipation for God's ultimate reality—appearing with Him in glory—begins to glow, making everything earthly pale in comparison. Earth's pain keeps crushing our hopes, reminding us this world can never, never satisfy us.

Only heaven can.

And every time we begin to nestle too comfortably on this planet, God racks open the locks of the dam to allow an ice-cold splash of suffering to wake us from our spiritual slumber.

The fact is, this world never was our true home. We've always been passing through. We've always been on our way Somewhere Else. We've always been "marching to Zion."

God wants us to march into the reality He has in mind for us, the only reality that ultimately counts. It requires gutsy faith to do so, but as we trust God, we move beyond the present into the future.

In fact, we create the very future God intends for us. We bring the joy of Zion, the happiness of heaven, right into the present tense.

> *The men of grace have found,*
> *Glory begun below.*
> *Celestial fruits on earthly ground*
> *Celestial fruits on earthly ground*
> *From faith and hope may grow,*
> *From faith and hope may grow.*

So we set our focus not on what is seen, but what is unseen. For what is seen is only temporary, but what is unseen is eternal.

And its price is far, far above rubies.

APPENDIX A

How Did Suffering Come into Our World?

In the beginning, God created the universe and gave the earth to man, appointing him as "assistant ruler" over the earth (Genesis 1:26). Adam and Eve ruled the earth under God's authority. There was no sin and, therefore, none of sin's awful results. Pollution was nonexistent. Nature was helpful, not hostile to man. No hurricanes, floods, tsunamis, tidal waves, or volcanic eruptions threatened man's survival. Death and disease were unknown. There was no fear that one of Eden's luscious-looking fruits might secretly contain some fatal poison. For both humans and the world of nature, it was truly paradise.

But at some point in this idyllic life on a perfect world, the evil one entered the scene. Satan, who had rebelled against God in a prideful struggle, followed by his army of demons, had set up a rival kingdom against God.

And planet earth became his headquarters. As C. S. Lewis imagined it, earth became "the silent planet," isolated and alone in the universe.

Mankind was enticed to sin, to eat the forbidden fruit, and as a result a curse fell upon man—and all of creation. (See Romans 8:20–23.) The whole realm of nature became subject to futility and frustration, to the endless cycle of change and decay. It seems quite possible that before this time, all animals may have been vegetarians. Now they fed upon one another, and violence brought about the law of the jungle.

Just as thorns and thistles attacked the earth, sickness and weakness attacked man's body. As we read through the book of Genesis, the human lifespan (once immortal) became shorter and shorter. No longer did people live hundreds of years as the early generations did. Illness and disease infested the world. Deformed babies and mentally-handicapped children became a fact of life.

And worst of all—the whole process ended in death.

Plants died.

Animals died.

People died.

Yes, sin brought its own special consequences and results. Satan became the king of planet earth, the "god of this age," the "ruler of the kingdom of the air," and the "prince of this world" (2 Corinthians 4:4; Ephesians 2:2; John 12:31).

Where then does disease come from?

Disease is just one of the many results of man's sin, along with death, sorrow, guilt, and disasters of nature.

Scripture on God's Control over Human Suffering[12]

All Christians acknowledge that God holds ultimate power in the universe. But does He always *exercise* it, especially when humans suffer? The causes behind human suffering are listed as major categories below. Under each are Scriptures asserting God's *active* (not merely reactive) control.

I. God exercises control over the inanimate forces of nature

A. Genesis 1:3: *And God said, "Let there be light," and there was light.*

B. Genesis 1:9: *And God said, "Let the water under the sky be gathered to one place, and let dry ground appear." And it was so.*

C. Genesis 1:11: *Then God said, "Let the land produce vegetation: seed-bearing plants and trees on the land that bear fruit with seed in it, according to their various kinds." And it was so.*

D. Genesis 6:17: *"I am going to bring floodwaters on the earth to destroy all life under the heavens, every creature that has the breath of life in it. Everything on earth will perish."*

E. Genesis 19:24–25: *Then the LORD rained down burning sulfur on Sodom and Gomorrah—from the LORD out of the heavens. Thus he overthrew those cities and the entire plain, including all those living in the cities—and also the vegetation in the land.*

F. Exodus 3:2: *There the angel of the LORD appeared to him in flames of fire from within a bush. Moses saw that though the bush was on fire it did not burn up.*

G. Exodus 9:23, 26: *When Moses stretched out his staff toward the sky, the LORD sent thunder and hail, and lightning flashed down to the ground. So the LORD rained hail on the land of Egypt. . . . The only place it did not hail was the land of Goshen, where the Israelites were.*

H. Exodus 10:21 – 23: *Then the LORD said to Moses, "Stretch out your hand toward the sky so that darkness will spread over Egypt—darkness that can be felt." So Moses stretched out his hand toward the sky, and total darkness covered all Egypt for three days. . . . Yet all the Israelites had light in the places where they lived.*

I. Exodus 14:21, 26 – 27: *Then Moses stretched out his hand over the sea, and all that night the LORD drove the sea back with a strong east wind and turned it into dry land. The waters were divided. . . . Then the LORD said to Moses, "Stretch out your hand over the sea so that the waters may flow back over the Egyptians and their chariots and horsemen." Moses stretched out his hand over the sea, and at daybreak the sea went back to its place. The Egyptians were fleeing toward it, and the LORD swept them into the sea.*

J. Numbers 16:28 – 33: *Then Moses said, "This is how you will know that the LORD has sent me to do all these things and that it was not my idea: If these men die a natural death and experience only what usually happens to men, then the LORD has not sent me. But if the LORD brings about something totally new, and the earth opens its mouth and swallows them, with everything that belongs to them, and they go down alive into the grave, then you will know that these men have treated the LORD with contempt." As soon as he finished saying all this, the ground under them split apart and the earth opened its mouth and swallowed them, with their households and all Korah's men and all their possessions. They went down alive into the grave, with everything they owned; the earth closed over them, and they perished and were gone from the community.*

K. Psalms 147:12, 15 – 18: *Extol the LORD, O Jerusalem; praise your God, O Zion. . . . He sends his command to the earth; his word runs swiftly. He spreads the snow like wool and scatters the frost like ashes. He hurls down his hail like pebbles. Who can withstand his icy blast?*

He sends his word and melts them; he stirs up his breezes, and the waters flow.

L. Amos 4:7 – 10: *"I also withheld rain from you when the harvest was still three months away. I sent rain on one town, but withheld it from another. One field had rain; another had none and dried up. People staggered from town to town for water but did not get enough to drink, yet you have not returned to me," declares the LORD. "Many times I struck your gardens and vineyards, I struck them with blight and mildew . . . yet you have not returned to me," declares the LORD.*

M. Jonah 1:4: *Then the LORD sent a great wind on the sea, and such a violent storm arose that the ship threatened to break up.*

N. Mark 4:36 – 41: *Leaving the crowd behind, they took him along, just as he was, in the boat. There were also other boats with him. A furious squall came up, and the waves broke over the boat, so that it was nearly swamped. . . . He got up, rebuked the wind and said to the waves, "Quiet! Be still!" Then the wind died down and it was completely calm. He said to his disciples, "Why are you so afraid? Do you still have no faith?" They were terrified and asked each other, "Who is this? Even the wind and the waves obey him!"*

II. God exercises control over the animal world (includes disease-causing micro-organisms)

A. Genesis 2:19: *Now the LORD God had formed out of the ground all the beasts of the field and all the birds of the air. He brought them to the man to see what he would name them. . . .*

B. Genesis 6:20: *Two of every kind of bird, of every kind of animal and of every kind of creature that moves along the ground will come to you to be kept alive.*

C. Exodus 8:1 – 2, 6: *Then the LORD said to Moses, "Go to Pharaoh and say to him, 'This is what the LORD says: Let my people go, so that they may worship me. If you refuse to let them go, I will plague your whole country with frogs.' " . . . So Aaron stretched out his hand over the waters of Egypt, and the frogs came up and covered the land.*

D. Exodus 8:20–21, 24, 30–31: *Then the LORD said to Moses, "Get up early in the morning and confront Pharaoh as he goes to the water and say to him, 'This is what the LORD says: Let my people go, so that they may worship me. If you do not let my people go, I will send swarms of flies on you. . . .' " And the LORD did this. Dense swarms of flies poured into Pharaoh's palace and into the houses of his officials, and throughout Egypt the land was ruined by the flies. . . . Then Moses left Pharaoh and prayed to the LORD, and the LORD did what Moses asked: The flies left Pharaoh and his officials and his people; not a fly remained.*

E. Exodus 10:13: *So Moses stretched out his staff over Egypt, and the LORD made an east wind blow across the land all that day and all that night. By morning the wind had brought the locusts.*

F. Numbers 22:28: *Then the LORD opened the donkey's mouth, and she said to Balaam, "What have I done to you to make you beat me these three times?"*

G. 1 Kings 17:2–4: *Then the word of the LORD came to Elijah: "Leave here, turn eastward and hide in the Kerith Ravine, east of the Jordan. You will drink from the brook, and I have ordered the ravens to feed you there."*

H. 2 Kings 17:25: *When they first lived there, they did not worship the LORD; so he sent lions among them and they killed some of the people.*

I. Jonah 1:17 cf. 2:10: *But the LORD provided a great fish to swallow Jonah. . . . And the LORD commanded the fish, and it vomited Jonah onto dry land.*

J. Jonah 4:6–7: *Then the LORD God provided a vine and made it grow up over Jonah to give shade for his head. . . . But at dawn the next day God provided a worm, which chewed the vine so that it withered.*

K. Matthew 17:27: *[Jesus speaking to Peter] "But so that we may not offend them, go to the lake and throw out your line. Take the first fish you catch; open its mouth and you will find a four-drachma coin. Take it and give it to them for my tax and yours."*

III. God exercises control over human tools and technology

A. Exodus 14:24–25: *During the last watch of the night the LORD looked down from the pillar of fire and cloud at the Egyptian army and threw it into confusion. He made the wheels of their chariots come off so that they had difficulty driving. And the Egyptians said, "Let's get away from the Israelites! The LORD is fighting for them against Egypt."*

B. 2 Kings 6:5–6: *As one of them was cutting down a tree, the iron ax head fell into the water. "Oh, my lord," he cried out, "it was borrowed!" The man of God asked, "Where did it fall?" When he showed him the place, Elisha cut a stick and threw it there, and made the iron float.*

C. 2 Chronicles 18:33–34: *[Setting: God has decreed that wicked King Ahab of Israel must die in battle. The prophet Micaiah delivers this message to Ahab, who ignores the prophet and goes to war anyway. The battle is described.] But someone drew his bow at random and hit the king of Israel between the sections of his armor. . . . All day long the battle raged, and the king of Israel propped himself up in his chariot facing the Arameans until evening. Then at sunset he died. [The point: God fulfilled his purpose to have Ahab killed in war by overseeing the path of an arrow shot "at random."]*

D. Proverbs 16:33: *The lot is cast into the lap, but its every decision is from the LORD.*

E. Daniel 3:27–28: *[Setting: Shadrach, Meshach, and Abednego are thrown into a blazing furnace by King Nebuchadnezzar for refusing to bow down to a golden image. The soldiers who throw them in are burned, but the three are unharmed. Amazed, the king calls for them to come out.] . . . The satraps, prefects, governors and royal advisers crowded around them. They saw that the fire had not harmed their bodies, nor was a hair of their heads singed; their robes were not scorched, and there was no smell of fire on them. Then Nebuchadnezzar said, "Praise be to the God of Shadrach, Meshach and Abednego, who has sent his angel and rescued his servants!"*

IV. God exercises control over the thoughts and actions of humans

A. The Bible clearly teaches that God governs even human beings, who have intelligence and a will of their own.

   1. Proverbs 16:9: *In his heart a man plans his course, but the LORD determines his steps.*

   2. Proverbs 19:21: *Many are the plans in a man's heart, but it is the LORD'S purpose that prevails.*

   3. Proverbs 20:24: *A man's steps are directed by the LORD. How then can anyone understand his own way?*

   4. Proverbs 21:1: *The king's heart is in the hand of the LORD; he directs it like a watercourse wherever he pleases.*

   5. Daniel 5:23: *[Daniel speaking to the pagan king Belshazzar] " . . . But you did not honor the God who holds in his hand your life and all your ways."*

B. Most Christians willingly acknowledge God as the ultimate source of all people's good deeds.

   1. Genesis 20:3–6: *[Abimelech, pagan king of Gerar, has taken Sarah, wife of Abraham, into his harem.] But God came to Abimelech in a dream one night and said to him, "You are as good as dead because of the woman you have taken; she is a married woman." Now Abimelech had not gone near her, so he said, "Lord, will you destroy an innocent nation? Did [her husband Abraham] not say to me, 'She is my sister,' and didn't she also say, 'He is my brother'? I have done this with a clear conscience and clean hands." Then God said to him in the dream, "Yes, I know you did this with a clear conscience, and so I have kept you from sinning against me. That is why I did not let you touch her."*

   2. 1 Samuel 25:32–33: *David said to Abigail, "Praise be to the LORD, the God of Israel, who has sent you today to meet me. May you be blessed for your good judgment and for keeping me from bloodshed this day and from avenging myself with my own hands."*

   3. Ezra 1:1: *In the first year of Cyrus king of Persia, in order to fulfill the word of the LORD spoken by Jeremiah, the LORD moved the*

heart of Cyrus king of Persia to make a proclamation throughout his realm and to put it in writing. [The Jewish exiles may return to Israel.]

4. Acts 16:14: *One of those listening was a woman named Lydia, a dealer in purple cloth from the city of Thyatira, who was a worshiper of God. The Lord opened her heart to respond to Paul's message.*

5. Romans 7:18: *I know that nothing good lives in me, that is, in my sinful nature. For I have the desire to do what is good, but I cannot carry it out. [The point: Human nature, left to itself, never chooses the truly good; it chooses good only when aided by God.]*

6. Philippians 2:13: *For it is God who works in you to will and to act according to his good purpose.*

7. 2 Corinthians 8:16: *I thank God, who put into the heart of Titus the same concern I have for you.*

C. But the Bible is equally clear that God controls even people's wicked, deluded actions. He is not the source of their wicked deeds, for James 1:13 says that God tempts no one. Rather, He sees to it that people give expression to their own sinful desires in such a way as to fulfill His plans unwittingly, not their own. He accomplishes this by infinite wisdom beyond our grasp.

1. Genesis 45:7–8: *[Joseph, to his brothers who sold him into slavery.] "But God sent me ahead of you to preserve for you a remnant on earth and to save your lives by a great deliverance. So then, it was not you who sent me here, but God. He made me father to Pharaoh, lord of his entire household and ruler of all Egypt."*

2. Exodus 4:21: *The LORD said to Moses, "When you return to Egypt, see that you perform before Pharaoh all the wonders I have given you the power to do. But I will harden his heart so that he will not let the people go." Cf. Romans 9:17: For the Scripture says to Pharaoh: "I raised you up for this very purpose, that I might display my power in you and that my name might be proclaimed in all the earth."*

3. Exodus 14:17: *"I will harden the hearts of the Egyptians so that they will go in after [the Israelites]. And I will gain glory through Pharaoh and all his army, through his chariots and his horsemen."*

4. Deuteronomy 2:30: *"But Sihon king of Heshbon refused to let us pass through. For the LORD your God had made his spirit stubborn and his heart obstinate in order to give him into your hands . . ."*

5. Joshua 11:19–20: *Except for the Hivites living in Gibeon, not one city made a treaty of peace with the Israelites, who took them all in battle. For it was the LORD himself who hardened their hearts to wage war against Israel, so that he might destroy them totally, exterminating them without mercy, as the LORD had commanded Moses.*

6. 2 Samuel 17:14: *Absalom and all the men of Israel said, "The advice of Hushai the Arkite is better than that of Ahithophel." For the LORD had determined to frustrate the good advice of Ahithophel in order to bring disaster on Absalom.*

7. 2 Kings 24:2–3: *The LORD sent Babylonian, Aramean, Moabite and Ammonite raiders against [King Jehoiakim]. He sent them to destroy Judah, in accordance with the word of the LORD proclaimed by his servants the prophets. Surely these things happened to Judah according to the Lord's command, in order to remove them from his presence because of the sins of Manasseh and all he had done.*

8. Psalm 105:25 NASB: *He turned [the Egyptians'] heart to hate His people. . . .*

9. Proverbs 16:4: *The LORD works out everything for his own ends — even the wicked for a day of disaster.*

10. Isaiah 10:5–7, 15: *[Setting: God is sending the wicked Assyrian armies to punish his people Israel, who have sinned so badly they are called "a godless nation."]*

> *Woe to the Assyrian, the rod of my anger,*
>> *in whose hand is the club of my wrath!*
> *I send him against a godless nation,*
>> *I dispatch him against a people who anger me,*
> *to seize loot and snatch plunder,*
>> *and to trample them down like mud in the streets.*

> But this is not what he [the Assyrian king] intends,
>> this is not what he has in mind;
> his purpose is to destroy,
>> to put an end to many nations. . . .
> Does the ax raise itself above him who swings it,
>> or the saw boast against him who uses it?
> As if a rod were to wield him who lifts it up,
>> or a club brandish him who is not wood!

11. Acts 4:27–28: [*The early Christians are addressing God.*] "Indeed Herod and Pontius Pilate met together with the Gentiles and the people of Israel in this city to conspire against your holy servant Jesus, whom you anointed. They did what your power and will had decided beforehand should happen."

12. 2 Thessalonians 2:11–12: *For this reason God sends them a powerful delusion so that they will believe the lie and so that all will be condemned who have not believed the truth but have delighted in wickedness.*

V. God exercises control even over Satan and demons

A. Judges 9:23: *God sent an evil spirit between Abimelech and the citizens of Shechem, who acted treacherously against Abimelech.*

B. 1 Samuel 16:14: *Now the Spirit of the LORD had departed from Saul, and an evil spirit from the LORD tormented him.*

C. 1 Kings 22:23: *So now the LORD has put a lying spirit in the mouths of all these prophets of yours. The LORD has decreed disaster for you.*

D. 1 Chronicles 21:1: *Satan rose up against Israel and incited David to take a census of Israel.* Cf. 2 Samuel 24:1: *Again the anger of the LORD burned against Israel, and he incited David against them, saying, "Go and take a census of Israel and Judah."*

E. Job 2:4–6 NASB: *Satan answered the LORD and said, " . . . Put forth Your hand now, and touch [Job's] bone and his flesh; he will curse You to Your face." So the LORD said to Satan, "Behold, he is in your power, only spare his life."* [*The point: Satan knew he could not touch*

Job without God decreeing it: "Put forth Thy hand." God assigns the harassing of Job to Satan, yet clearly defines the limits beyond which he cannot operate: "Behold, he is in your power, only spare his life."]

F. Matthew 4:10–11: *Jesus said to him, "Away from me, Satan! . . ." Then the devil left him. . . .*

G. Mark 1:23–27: *Just then a man in their synagogue who was possessed by an evil spirit cried out, "What do you want with us, Jesus of Nazareth? Have you come to destroy us? I know who you are — the Holy One of God!" "Be quiet!" said Jesus sternly. "Come out of him!" The evil spirit shook the man violently and came out of him with a shriek. The people were all so amazed that they asked each other, "What is this? A new teaching — and with authority! He even gives orders to evil spirits and they obey him."*

H. Luke 22:31: *"Simon, Simon, Satan has asked to sift you as wheat . . ."* [The point: Satan would not ask for permission if the power was already his, for it is not his nature to limit his actions simply to avoid displeasing God.]

I. John 12:37–40: *Even after Jesus had done all these miraculous signs in their presence, they still would not believe in him. This was to fulfill the word of Isaiah the prophet: "Lord, who has believed our message and to whom has the arm of the Lord been revealed?" For this reason they could not believe, because, as Isaiah says elsewhere: "He has blinded their eyes and deadened their hearts, so they can neither see with their eyes, nor understand with their hearts, nor turn — and I would heal them."* Cf. 2 Corinthians 4:4: *The god of this age* [i.e., Satan] *has blinded the minds of unbelievers, so that they cannot see the light of the gospel of the glory of Christ. . . .*

VI. In summary, God exercises control over all beings, things, and actions

A. Exodus 4:11: *The LORD said to him, "Who gave man his mouth? Who makes him deaf or mute? Who gives him sight or makes him blind? Is it not I, the LORD?"*

B. Job 42:2: *"I know that you can do all things; no plan of yours can be thwarted."*

C. Psalms 33:10–11: *The LORD foils the plans of the nations; he thwarts the purposes of the peoples. But the plans of the LORD stand firm forever, the purposes of his heart through all generations.*

D. Psalms 115:3: *Our God is in heaven; he does whatever pleases him.*

E. Lamentations 3:38: *Is it not from the mouth of the Most High that both calamities and good things come?*

F. Isaiah 14:27: *For the LORD Almighty has purposed, and who can thwart him? His hand is stretched out, and who can turn it back?*

G. Isaiah 45:7: *"I form the light and create darkness, I bring prosperity and create disaster; I, the LORD, do all these things."*

H. Daniel 4:35: *He does as he pleases with the powers of heaven and the peoples of the earth. No one can hold back his hand or say to him: "What have you done?"*

I. Amos 3:6: *When disaster comes to a city, has not the LORD caused it?*

J. Ephesians 1:11: *In him we were also chosen, having been predestined according to the plan of him who works out everything in conformity with the purpose of his will.*

K. 1 Thessalonians 3:3: *You know quite well that we were destined for [trials].*

—

In conclusion, God decrees all things, even human suffering, but Satan often is the messenger of those decrees even as he fights against the God who issued them. When Satan, evil people, or "accidents" of any kind bring trials upon us, we can answer with Joseph to his brothers who sold him into slavery, "As for you, you meant evil against me, but God meant it for good" (Genesis 50:20 NASB).

Scripture on God's Purpose in Our Sufferings

Discovering God's hand in hardship is really a discovery of God's Word. The following verses underscore a few of the benefits derived from our pain and problems. These power-packed passages serve as a lens through which we may gain a clearer perspective on our afflictions.

Suffering is used to increase our awareness of the sustaining power of God to whom we owe our sustenance.

Psalm 68:19: *Praise be to the Lord, to God our Savior, who daily bears our burdens.*

God uses suffering to refine, perfect, strengthen, and keep us from falling.

Psalm 66:8–9: *Praise our God, O peoples, let the sound of his praise be heard; he has preserved our lives and kept our feet from slipping.*

Hebrews 2:10: *In bringing many sons to glory, it was fitting that God, for whom and through whom everything exists, should make the author of their salvation perfect through suffering.*

Suffering allows the life of Christ to be manifested in our mortal flesh.

2 Corinthians 4:7–11: *But we have this treasure in jars of clay to show that this all-surpassing power is from God and not from us. We are hard pressed on every side, but not crushed; perplexed, but not in despair; persecuted, but not abandoned; struck down, but not destroyed.*

We always carry around in our body the death of Jesus, so that the life of Jesus may also be revealed in our body. For we who are alive are always being given over to death for Jesus' sake, so that his life may be revealed in our mortal body.

Suffering bankrupts us, making us dependent on God.

2 Corinthians 12:9: *"My grace is sufficient for you, for my power is made perfect in weakness." Therefore I will boast all the more gladly about my weaknesses, so that Christ's power may rest on me.*

Suffering teaches us humility.

2 Corinthians 12:7: *To keep me from becoming conceited because of these surpassingly great revelations, there was given me a thorn in my flesh, a messenger of Satan, to torment me.*

Suffering imparts the mind of Christ.

Philippians 2:1–11: *If you have any encouragement from being united with Christ, if any comfort from his love, if any fellowship with the Spirit, if any tenderness and compassion, then make my joy complete by being like-minded, having the same love, being one in spirit and purpose. Do nothing out of selfish ambition or vain conceit, but in humility consider others better than yourselves. Each of you should look not only to your own interests, but also to the interests of others. Your attitude should be the same as that of Christ Jesus: Who, being in very nature God, did not consider equality with God something to be grasped, but made himself nothing, taking the very nature of a servant, being made in human likeness. And being found in appearance as a man, he humbled himself and became obedient to death—even death on a cross! Therefore God exalted him to the highest place and gave him the name that is above every name, that at the name of Jesus every knee should bow, in heaven and on earth and under the earth, and every tongue confess that Jesus Christ is Lord, to the glory of God the Father.*

Suffering teaches us that God is more concerned with character than comfort.

Romans 5:3–4: *Not only so, but we also rejoice in our sufferings, because we know that suffering produces perseverance; perseverance, character; and character, hope.*

Hebrews 12:10–11: *Our fathers disciplined us for a little while as they thought best; but God disciplines us for our good, that we may share in his holiness. No discipline seems pleasant at the time, but painful. Later on, however, it produces a harvest of righteousness and peace for those who have been trained by it.*

Suffering teaches us that the greatest good of the Christian life is not absence of pain but Christ-likeness.

2 Corinthians 4:8–10: *We are hard pressed on every side, but not crushed; perplexed, but not in despair; persecuted, but not abandoned; struck down, but not destroyed. We always carry around in our body the death of Jesus, so that the life of Jesus may also be revealed in our body.*

Romans 8:28–29: *And we know that in all things God works for the good of those who love him, who have been called according to his purpose. For those God foreknew he also predestined to be conformed to the likeness of his Son, that he might be the firstborn among many brothers.*

Suffering can be a chastisement from God for sin and rebellion.

Psalm 107:17: *Some became fools through their rebellious ways and suffered affliction because of their iniquities.*

Obedience and self-control is learned from suffering.

Hebrews 5:8: *Although he was a son, he learned obedience from what he suffered.*

Psalm 119:67: *Before I was afflicted I went astray, but now I obey your word.*

Romans 5:1–5: *Therefore, since we have been justified through faith, we have peace with God through our Lord Jesus Christ, through whom we have gained access by faith into this grace in which we now stand. And we rejoice in the hope of the glory of God. Not only so, but we also rejoice in our sufferings, because we know that suffering produces perseverance; perseverance, character; and character, hope. And hope does not disappoint us, because God has poured out his love into our hearts by the Holy Spirit, whom he has given us.*

James 1:2–8: *Consider it pure joy, my brothers, whenever you face trials of many kinds, because you know that the testing of your faith develops perseverance. Perseverance must finish its work so that you may be mature and complete, not lacking anything. If any of you lacks wisdom, he should ask God, who gives generously to all without finding fault, and it will be given to him. But when he asks, he must believe and not doubt, because he who doubts is like a wave of the sea, blown and tossed by the wind. That man should not think he will receive anything from the Lord; he is a double-minded man, unstable in all he does.*

Philippians 3:10: *I want to know Christ and the power of his resurrection and the fellowship of sharing in his sufferings, becoming like him in his death.*

Voluntary suffering is one way to demonstrate the love of God.

2 Corinthians 8:1–2, 9: *And now, brothers, we want you to know about the grace that God has given the Macedonian churches. Out of the most severe trial, their overflowing joy and their extreme poverty welled up in rich generosity . . . For you know the grace of our Lord Jesus Christ, that though he was rich, yet for your sakes he became poor, so that you through his poverty might become rich.*

Suffering is part of the struggle against sin.

Hebrews 12:4–13: *In your struggle against sin, you have not yet resisted to the point of shedding your blood. And you have forgotten that word of encouragement that addresses you as sons: "My son, do not* make light of the Lord's discipline, and do not lose heart when he rebukes you, because the Lord disciplines those he loves, and he punishes everyone he accepts as a son." Endure hardship as discipline; God is treating you as sons. For what son is not disciplined by his father? If you are not disciplined (and everyone undergoes discipline), then you are illegitimate children and not true sons. Moreover, we have all had human fathers who disciplined us and we respected them for it. How much more should we submit to the Father of our spirits and live! Our fathers disciplined us for a little while as they thought best; but God disciplines us for our good, that we may share in his holiness. No discipline seems pleasant at the time, but painful. Later on, however, it produces a harvest of righteousness and peace for those who have been trained by it. Therefore, strengthen your feeble arms and weak knees. "Make level paths for your feet," so that the lame may not be disabled, but rather healed.

Suffering is part of the struggle against evil men.

Psalm 27:12: *Do not turn me over to the desire of my foes, for false witnesses rise up against me, breathing out violence.*

Psalm 37:14 – 15: *The wicked draw the sword and bend the bow to bring down the poor and needy, to slay those whose ways are upright. But their swords will pierce their own hearts, and their bows will be broken.*

Suffering is part of the struggle for the kingdom of God.

2 Thessalonians 1:5: *All this is evidence that God's judgment is right, and as a result you will be counted worthy of the kingdom of God, for which you are suffering.*

Suffering is part of the struggle for the Gospel.

2 Timothy 2:8 – 9: *This is my gospel, for which I am suffering even to the point of being chained like a criminal. But God's word is not chained.*

Suffering is part of the struggle against injustice.

1 Peter 2:19: *For it is commendable if a man bears up under the pain of unjust suffering because he is conscious of God.*

Suffering is part of the struggle for the name of Christ.

Acts 5:41: *The apostles left the Sanhedrin, rejoicing because they had been counted worthy of suffering disgrace for the Name.*

1 Peter 4:14: *If you are insulted because of the name of Christ, you are blessed, for the Spirit of glory and of God rests on you.*

Suffering indicates how the righteous become sharers in Christ's suffering.

2 Corinthians 1:5: *For just as the sufferings of Christ flow over into our lives, so also through Christ our comfort overflows.*

1 Peter 4:12–13: *Dear friends, do not be surprised at the painful trial you are suffering, as though something strange were happening to you. But rejoice that you participate in the sufferings of Christ, so that you may be overjoyed when his glory is revealed.*

Endurance of suffering is given as a cause for reward.

2 Corinthians 4:17: *For our light and momentary troubles are achieving for us an eternal glory that far outweighs them all.*

2 Timothy 2:12: *If we endure, we will also reign with him. If we disown him, he will also disown us.*

Suffering forces community and the administration of our gifts for the common good.

Philippians 4:12–15: *I know what it is to be in need, and I know what it is to have plenty. I have learned the secret of being content in any and every situation, whether well fed or hungry, whether living in plenty or in want. I can do everything through him who gives me strength. Yet it was good of you to share in my troubles. Moreover, as you Philippians know, in the early days of your acquaintance with the gospel, when I set out from Macedonia, not one church shared with me in the matter of giving and receiving, except you only.*

Suffering binds Christians together into a common or joint purpose.

Revelation 1:9: *I, John, your brother and companion in the suffering and kingdom and patient endurance that are ours in Jesus, was on the island of Patmos because of the word of God and the testimony of Jesus.*

Suffering produces discernment, knowledge, and teaches us God's statutes.

Psalm 119:66–67, 71: *Teach me knowledge and good judgment, for I believe in your commands. Before I was afflicted I went astray, but now I obey your word . . . It was good for me to be afflicted so that I might learn your decrees.*

Through suffering, God is able to obtain our broken and contrite spirit, which he desires.

Psalm 51:16–17: *You do not delight in sacrifice, or I would bring it; you do not take pleasure in burnt offerings. The sacrifices of God are a broken spirit; a broken and contrite heart, O God, you will not despise.*

Suffering causes us to discipline our minds by making us focus our hope on the grace to be revealed at the revelation of Jesus Christ.

1 Peter 1:6, 13: *In this you greatly rejoice, though now for a little while you may have had to suffer grief in all kinds of trials . . . Therefore, prepare your minds for action; be self-controlled; set your hope fully on the grace to be given you when Jesus Christ is revealed.*

God uses suffering to humble us so he can exalt us at the proper time.

1 Peter 5:6–7: *Humble yourselves, therefore, under God's mighty hand, that he may lift you up in due time. Cast all your anxiety on him because he cares for you.*

Suffering teaches us to number our days so we can present to God a heart of wisdom.

> Psalm 90:7–12: *We are consumed by your anger and terrified by your indignation. You have set our iniquities before you, our secret sins in the light of your presence. All our days pass away under your wrath; we finish our years with a moan. The length of our days is seventy years—or eighty, if we have the strength; yet their span is but trouble and sorrow, for they quickly pass, and we fly away. Who knows the power of your anger? For your wrath is as great as the fear that is due you. Teach us to number our days aright, that we may gain a heart of wisdom.*

Suffering is sometimes necessary to win the lost.

> 2 Timothy 2:8–10: *Remember Jesus Christ, raised from the dead, descended from David. This is my gospel, for which I am suffering even to the point of being chained like a criminal. But God's word is not chained. Therefore I endure everything for the sake of the elect, that they too may obtain the salvation that is in Christ Jesus, with eternal glory.*

> 2 Timothy 4:5–6: *But you, keep your head in all situations, endure hardship, do the work of an evangelist, discharge all the duties of your ministry. For I am already being poured out like a drink offering, and the time has come for my departure.*

Suffering strengthens and allows us to comfort others who are weak.

> 2 Corinthians 1:3–11: *Praise be to the God and Father of our Lord Jesus Christ, the Father of compassion and the God of all comfort, who comforts us in all our troubles, so that we can comfort those in any trouble with the comfort we ourselves have received from God. For just as the sufferings of Christ flow over into our lives, so also through Christ our comfort overflows. If we are distressed, it is for your comfort and salvation; if we are comforted, it is for your comfort, which*

produces in you patient endurance of the same sufferings we suffer. And our hope for you is firm, because we know that just as you share in our sufferings, so also you share in our comfort. We do not want you to be uninformed, brothers, about the hardships we suffered in the province of Asia. We were under great pressure, far beyond our ability to endure, so that we despaired even of life. Indeed, in our hearts we felt the sentence of death. But this happened that we might not rely on ourselves but on God, who raises the dead. He has delivered us from such a deadly peril, and he will deliver us. On him we have set our hope that he will continue to deliver us, as you help us by your prayers. Then many will give thanks on our behalf for the gracious favor granted us in answer to the prayers of many.

Suffering is small compared to the surpassing value of knowing Christ.

Philippians 3:8: *What is more, I consider everything a loss compared to the surpassing greatness of knowing Christ Jesus my Lord, for whose sake I have lost all things. I consider them rubbish, that I may gain Christ.*

God desires truth in our innermost being, and one way he does it is through suffering.

Psalm 51:6: *Surely you desire truth in the inner parts; you teach me wisdom in the inmost place.*

Psalm 119:17: *Do good to your servant, and I will live; I will obey your word.*

The equity for suffering will be found in the next life.

Psalm 58:10 – 11: *The righteous will be glad when they are avenged, when they bathe their feet in the blood of the wicked. Then men will say, "Surely the righteous still are rewarded; surely there is a God who judges the earth."*

Suffering is always coupled with a greater source of grace.

2 Timothy 1:7–8: *For God did not give us a spirit of timidity, but a spirit of power, of love and of self-discipline. So do not be ashamed to testify about our Lord, or ashamed of me his prisoner. But join with me in suffering for the gospel, by the power of God.*

2 Timothy 4:16–18: *At my first defense, no one came to my support, but everyone deserted me. May it not be held against them. But the Lord stood at my side and gave me strength, so that through me the message might be fully proclaimed and all the Gentiles might hear it. And I was delivered from the lion's mouth. The Lord will rescue me from every evil attack and will bring me safely to his heavenly kingdom. To him be glory for ever and ever. Amen.*

Suffering teaches us to give thanks in times of sorrow.

1 Thessalonians 5:18: *Give thanks in all circumstances.*

2 Corinthians 1:11: *Then many will give thanks on our behalf for the gracious favor granted us in answer to the prayers of many.*

Suffering increases faith.

Jeremiah 29:11: *"For I know the plans I have for you," declares the LORD, "plans to prosper you and not to harm you, plans to give you hope and a future."*

Suffering allows God to manifest his care.

Psalm 56:8: *Record my lament; list my tears on your scroll—are they not in your record?*

Suffering stretches our hope.

Job 13:14–15: *Why do I put myself in jeopardy and take my life in my hands? Though he slay me, yet will I hope in him; I will surely defend my ways to his face.*

Notes

1. J. I. Packer, *Hot Tub Religion* (Wheaton, Ill.: Tyndale, 1987), 192–93.
2. J. I. Packer, *Knowing God* (Downers Grove, Ill.: InterVarsity, 1973), 227.
3. Ibid.
4. From Barnes' Notes, Electronic Database Copyright © 1997, 2003 by Biblesoft, Inc. All rights reserved.
5. Edythe Draper, *Draper's Book of Quotations for the Christian World* (Wheaton, Ill.: Tyndale, 1992), 480.
6. Portions of this story are taken from Joni Eareckson Tada and Steven Estes, *When God Weeps* (Grand Rapids: Zondervan, 1997), 125.
7. Augustine, *Confessions*, I:1.
8. William Herbert Carruth, "Each in His Own Tongue," from *Each in His Own Tongue and Other Poems* (New York: P. F. Volland, c. 1920). Originally published as "A Poem" in *The British Journal of Nursing* (March 25, 1905).
9. Patrick Kavanaugh, *Spiritual Lives of Great Composers* (Grand Rapids: Zondervan, 1992, 1996), 75.
10. Thanks to Steve Estes for the wording of this last thought.
11. Tim Stafford, *Knowing the Face of God* (Colorado Springs: NavPress, 1996), 221.
12. Adapted from Appendix A of Joni Eareckson Tada and Steven Estes, *When God Weepss*.

In Closing ...

Thank you for taking time to journey with me through these pages. But there's so much more to say. And so many more people I would love for you to meet — people who are struggling through many challenges, yet are coming out on the other side filled with peace, power, and a godly perspective.

This is why I encourage you to visit us at the Joni and Friends International Disability Center. Our staff and volunteers provide exceptional programs and services for families affected by disability, not to mention disability ministry training in churches across the country. If you or a family member are struggling to come to grips with an injury or illness, I invite you to contact us and learn more about the practical and spiritual help which can be yours today.

Because no one — absolutely no one — should suffer alone. It's why God created spiritual community. And it's why our goal at the Joni and Friends International Disability Center is to help people like *you*.

Joni and Friends International Disability Center
P.O. Box 3333
Agoura Hills, CA 91376
818/707 – 5664
www.joniandfriends.org

Acknowledgments

My deepest thanks to Robert Wolgemuth and the team at *Wolgemuth & Associates* for opening new doors so I can share the many things I keep learning from my wheelchair and God's Word. I am so grateful for Larry Libby, my friend and fellow wordsmith from whom I am learning to slow down and write with my heart. And, finally, special thanks to the Zondervan family and to John Sloan for his unflagging support and enthusiasm. I may not have "hands" to write, but I have the willing and happy hands of these dear friends; for that, I am truly thankful.

A Lifetime of Wisdom

Embracing How
God Heals You

Joni Eareckson Tada

"Thank you, God, for this chair!"

Not the words you'd expect from a
woman who has spent forty years as a quadriplegic following a
tragic diving accident at seventeen. But it is the perspective of a
woman who has suffered heartbreaking losses ... and incomparable gains. Chief among those gains have been the insights she's
gained into the wisdom and nature of God—learned and refined
through seasons of difficulty and trial.

In one sense, that wisdom did cost Joni all she had: her hopes,
her dreams, her independence, her health, her freedom, and mobility. In the early years, it seemed a price much too high to pay.
But through four decades Joni's moved from enduring her circumstances to finding God's joy in them. And now she has written
a book that shares the heavenly wisdom and perspective she's
learned.

Many books have been written about tragedy and struggle, of
pain and bitterness, but in this book, Joni chooses to dwell not on
what she has lost but on what she has found.

Audio CD, Unabridged: 978-0-310-28953-1

Pick up a copy today at your favorite bookstore!

Pearls of Great Price

366 Daily Devotional Readings

Joni Eareckson Tada

Joni Eareckson Tada wants to help you become rich in faith and wealthy in hope. Some people focus on material treasures, but Joni reminds you that life's true gems come from God—priceless pearls that are worth everything to purchase ... and own.

In the tradition of *Diamonds in the Dust* and *More Precious Than Silver* comes this book, *Pearls of Great Price*. Written by a remarkable woman who has known firsthand God's faithfulness in the midst of indescribable difficulties, these 366 inspiring devotions, each filled with Joni's signature storytelling, will touch your soul like a genuine pearl—rare, beautiful, and precious.

To wake up each morning is, for Joni, to need the Lord Jesus desperately and to feel His blessing. And she yearns to help you grasp this blessing for yourself. Not a day breaks when she doesn't cling to God, asking for a fresh touch from heaven as well as a fresh view on His Word. It's the reason for her life. It's the reason why she writes. *Pearls of Great Price* so clearly depicts Joni's passion.

Allow these 366 meditations to uncover a wealth of promise, of eternal truths waiting to transform the events of your life into opportunities to catch and reflect God's glory. Featuring Joni's own beautiful line drawings, *Pearls of Great Price* will open your eyes and your heart to an abundance of blessings.

Hardcover, Jacketed: 978-0-310-26298-5

Pick up a copy today at your favorite bookstore!

The God I Love

A Lifetime of Walking with Jesus

Joni Eareckson Tada

The God I Love offers the eternal perspective of a woman in a wheelchair who affirms that the God she knows and loves is the center, the peacemaker, the passport to adventure, the joy ride, and the answer to her deepest longings.

Raised in an active, adventurous family, Joni Eareckson Tada worked hard and played hard to keep up with her older sisters and athletic father—until one day a diving accident left her a quadriplegic. But the tragedy that could have ended her life was in reality the beginning of an amazing, constantly unfolding story of grace that has touched the lives of millions worldwide and brought Joni unexpected joy and fulfillment.

Written with beauty, feeling, and amazing honesty, *The God I Love* captures the heart and soul of one woman's powerful, deeply personal journey of hope. It is a sojourn from a naïve child's belief to a tempered faith that transforms and transcends personal tragedy, bringing light to the darkest places and good out of the most difficult situations, and offering glimpses of the glory that awaits God's children.

Hardcover, Jacketed: 978-0-310-24008-2

Pick up a copy today at your favorite bookstore!

Joni

An Unforgettable Story

Joni Eareckson Tada

The award-winning story of a young woman who triumphed over devastating odds to touch countless lives the world over with the healing message of Christ. Includes photos and illustrations by Joni.

In a split second on a hot July afternoon, a diving accident transformed the life of Joni Eareckson Tada forever. She went from being an active young woman to facing every day in a wheelchair. In this unforgettable autobiography, Joni reveals each step of her struggle to accept her disability and discover the meaning of her life. The hard-earned truths she discovers and the special ways God reveals His love are testimonies to faith's triumph over hardship and suffering.

The 25th Anniversary edition of this award-winning story — which has more than 3,000,000 copies in print in over forty languages — will introduce a new generation of readers to the incredible greatness of God's power and mercy at work in those who fully give their hearts and lives to Him.

Joni has written an afterword in which she describes the events that have occurred in her life since the book's publication in 1976, including her marriage to Ken Tada and the expansion of her worldwide ministry to families affected by disability.

Joni is also available in an unabridged audio download version read by the author.

Softcover: 978-0-310-24001-3   Audio download, unabridged: 978-0-310-26158-2

Pick up a copy today at your favorite bookstore!

Share Your Thoughts

With the Author: Your comments will be forwarded to the author when you send them to *zauthor@zondervan.com*.

With Zondervan: Submit your review of this book by writing to *zreview@zondervan.com*.

Free Online Resources at
www.zondervan.com/hello

 Zondervan AuthorTracker: Be notified whenever your favorite authors publish new books, go on tour, or post an update about what's happening in their lives.

 Daily Bible Verses and Devotions: Enrich your life with daily Bible verses or devotions that help you start every morning focused on God.

 Free Email Publications: Sign up for newsletters on fiction, Christian living, church ministry, parenting, and more.

 Zondervan Bible Search: Find and compare Bible passages in a variety of translations at www.zondervanbiblesearch.com.

 Other Benefits: Register yourself to receive online benefits like coupons and special offers, or to participate in research.

ZONDERVAN®
.com